Thirty Thousand Days is a beauti
days matter. Even in the contexts
staggeringly challenging to mainta
that is needed in a life sold out to t
you will be taken through a journey that is all too common ... ...
plight we all can resonate with. Catherine weaves seamlessly between
the words of the Lord and her own personal narrative to draw us near
to the Almighty. The effects of her book are already building in our
hearts on how the Lord would have us grow closer to Him. Be warned
– this book will not leave you the same! Your eyes will shift toward
the eternal, your heart will align with His, and your love for people
will be the overflow.

D & S
Missionaries to North Africa

Thirty Thousand Days is beseeching us to live a life shaped by the
eternity that awaits those who trust Jesus. In these pages, Catherine
Morgan demonstrates a grasp of the Kingdom of God, and she has
the life to back it up.

Jay Williams
Pastor, Faith Baptist Church
Peshtigo, Wisconsin

This book is the culmination of years of God's work in Catherine
Morgan's life. Her writing reveals her passion for God's people to live
purposefully this side of eternity as they long for their eternal home.

Erika Blaine
Pastor's Wife,
Aurora, Colorado

I have nothing but praise for *Thirty Thousand Days*! I relished the
truths in this must-read book. Catherine's words challenged me to
live now focused on eternity. Time is short and there is great purpose
for each day God gives us!

Jen McShea
Stay-at-Home Mom
Greensboro, North Carolina

Catherine Morgan has an eloquent yet down-to-earth literary style and her book is one I want to read over and over again! It challenged and encouraged me to think bigger, deeper, bolder about the way my faith plays out in my daily life. She incorporates personal stories and accounts that are rich in detail and draw the reader in. She provides a unique perspective from her own life experiences that sets *Thirty Thousand Days* apart from other books in the same genre. It is an engaging read and one that propels the reader to view every day, every hour, every minute of this life in terms of its eternal significance.

Laurie Morgan
Lawyer
Dallas, Texas

Catherine Morgan views the world with an eternal perspective. She uses every day encounters to teach lessons filled with biblical truths to help share the message of salvation. She inspires others to walk with Jesus daily and seek His will. She is grounded in her faith and her writing is filled with hope, encouragement, and challenges for seekers and believers.

Karen Hoar
Stay-at-Home Mom
Birmingham, Alabama

Thirty Thousand Days — a tiny dot on the line of our lives for eternity. How do we spend those days, no, how do we invest those days? Catherine Morgan passionately and creatively guides us in the true journey of a life that matters, that counts, that satisfies. She calls us to love God and love others, just as Jesus did. And she helps us grab hold of a vision that will sustain us — an eternal perspective for the days of our lives.

Judy Douglass
Author of *Letters to My Children: Secrets of Success*

The Journey
Home to God

THIRTY THOUSAND DAYS

Catherine L. Morgan

CHRISTIAN
FOCUS

Unless otherwise indicated, Scripture quotations are from The Holy Bible, English Standard Version, copyright © 2001 by Crossway Bibles, a publishing ministry of Good News Publishers. Used by permission. All rights reserved. ESV Text Edition: 2011.

Scripture quotations marked NIV are taken from the HOLY BIBLE, NEW INTERNATIONAL VERSION. Copyright © 1973, 1978, 1984 by International Bible Society.Used by permission of Hodder & Stoughton Publishers, A member of the Hodder Headline Group. All rights reserved. "NIV" is a registered trademark of International Bible Society. UK trademark number 1448790.

Scripture quotations marked NASB are taken from the New American Standard Bible®, Copyright © 1960, 1962, 1963, 1968, 1971, 1972, 1973, 1975, 1977, 1995 by The Lockman Foundation © Used by Permission. (www.Lockman.org)

Scripture quotations marked MSG are taken from The Message. Copyright 1993, 1994, 1995, 1996, 2000, 2001, 2002. Used by permission of NavPress Publishing Group.

Scripture quotations marked (NLT) are taken from the Holy Bible, New Living Translation, copyright © 1996. Used by permission of Tyndale House Publishers, Inc., Wheaton, Illinois 60189. All rights reserved.

Scripture quotations marked RV are taken from the Revised Version (RV).

Catherine L Morgan lives in Colorado with three kids, two dogs and a yellow canoe. She and her husband, Michael, served on staff with Here's Life Inner City (a division of Cru) for several years and planted a church a decade ago. They are amazingly still standing! You can follow her blog at catherinesletters.com.

Copyright © Catherine L. Morgan 2016

paperback ISBN: 978-1-78191-783-1
epub ISBN: 978-1-78191-912-5
mobi ISBN: 978-1-78191-913-2

10 9 8 7 6 5 4 3 2 1

Published in 2016 by
Christian Focus Publications Ltd,
Geanies House, Fearn,
Ross-shire, IV20 1TW, Scotland.
www.christianfocus.com

Cover design by Pete Barnsley, Creative Hoot

Printed and bound by Bell and Bain, Glasgow

CONTENTS

Preface

No one has yet believed in God and the kingdom of God, no one has yet heard about the realm of the resurrected, and not been homesick from that hour, waiting and looking forward joyfully to being released from bodily existence.

— Dietrich Bonhoeffer

Late one night in the 1940s, a solitary train rattled down the track. Bound from Chicago, Illinois, it swayed along over bridges and through tunnels, heading always south, the steady chugging rhythm rocking families to sleep in the passenger cars. A few night owls, perhaps, sat up in the dining section, drinking coffee and reading the newspaper. A few porters wandered the aisles, keeping watch over the travelers under their care.

No one was likely to notice Aiden Wilson Tozer, a middle-aged pastor who took the train because he never owned a car. While others slept or joked or read, Tozer quietly created a masterpiece. In the one night it took to travel from Illinois to Texas, A.W. Tozer dashed off the first draft of a modern Christian classic, *The Pursuit of God*.

Tozer was under no illusion as he sat in the speeding locomotive that he'd arrived at his destination. He knew when he paid his ticket that his journey would be short, and he did not spend those few hours despairing, or asking as children inevitably do, 'are we there yet?' Although he was not home yet, Tozer's thoughts were trained on heaven, his heart fully absorbed in Someone he could not see there on the train.

All the days of our lives play out far from home. We awaken to life in a broken world, never to experience Eden until we breathe our last. We none of us know how many days we'll be given on this earth. Yet, for the length of days we're granted, we either stockpile treasure on earth or focus our homesick hearts on our ultimate destination.

Jesus Himself lived just thirty-three years, long enough to gather a dozen disciples and flip the world upside down. Always, Jesus remained an alien and a stranger in our world. With a perfectly eternal perspective, He remembered that He was not home yet.

Most of us will outlive Jesus by a fair stretch. The average human being lives not thirty years, but closer to 30,000 days. It's not long, but it is enough.

How have you spent your days? Maybe you're in college, dreaming about what's next. Perhaps you are a parent, and wrangle a half-dozen Mini-Mes off to school day after day. You might be mayor of your town, manager of your office, or ringmaster of a circus. Whether you have discovered a new planet or watched 30,000 hours of television, you're bound to have a nagging feeling that something in your world is not right. Why the long face?

You're homesick for a better country.

You're headed home on a rattle-trap train.

We're not home yet, but we're well on the way. Soon and very soon the train will pull into the station. What a sight awaits us when it does.

Introduction: Live abundantly

*The thief comes only to steal
and kill and destroy.
I came that they may have life and have it
abundantly.*

– John 10:10

I was about nine years old, heading into fourth grade. My best friend, who hadn't moved away yet, was climbing the swing set in my backyard with me, and I was being typically bossy.

'But there's a lake. And canoes. And a ropes course.'

'I don't care.'

'But Mary Beth. It will be so fun. We get to sleep in boxcars. Boxcars! Like *The Boxcar Children*.'[1]

---

1. A children's series begun by Gertrude Chandler Warner in 1924, published by Rand McNally. Still a popular children's

'I don't want to.'

'Why? Because you'll be homesick?' I was openly taunting her now, bullying, really. How could she be so childish? 'It's only for a week! A week with all kids and no parents!'

'I said I don't want to!'

'You're being dumb!' I shouted stubbornly, freckles blazing. 'Why would you be homesick at camp?' I was furious. What kind of kid turns down a week at camp with her best friend because she might miss home? And if she refused to go with me, then I really would be all alone.

All alone. Now that was a scary thought. And when eventually I cried myself to sleep on the first night of camp – desperately, foolishly homesick – Mary Beth was home sleeping in her own bed, happy as a clam. Neither of us knew that she'd be moving away in a matter of months, that my confident superiority would vanish like smoke without her by my side, that she would be making new friends in a far away town, gone not for a week, but permanently. And when the week of camp ended and I cried to leave (all traces of homesickness having washed away in the green lake) I had no idea what ache would linger for the rest of my life.

It comes and goes, that ache, a nameless longing, unnoticed as the rising tide, but deep. It is almost imperceptible, almost outside of the range of my poor hearing, but there it is – now a whisper, now

---

franchise with new releases up through 2016. "Boxcar" is an American word for train carriage.

a roar, and always singing, always taunting, always calling my name, singing me home.

I have felt it since I was a child. I do not belong here. I am an alien, a sojourner. This place is foreign to me, and though sometimes it reminds me of home, more often it is slightly toxic. I am ET, breathing strange fumes. I need to phone home.

But here I am, here we all are, stranded on this hostile planet, waiting. Longing. Maybe you feel it, too. Maybe, stuck in traffic, you realize that you feel equally stuck in life. Alone, maybe, or just out of place. The things you've given your life to don't seem to amount to much. You can't remember how you spent yesterday, or what it was you wanted to be doing at this age. Maybe what you've waited for your whole life has never come to pass, or when it did, it wasn't what you expected. Maybe your life has been one heartbreak after another, or maybe, if you've had a happy life, you live with a vague fear that it just won't last. Although the waiting seems interminable, there are reminders that in truth, our lives are short. A healthy older man, chopping trees one day, struck down with cancer the next. A young mother, collapsed on the cold tile floor after a spider bite. A baby, slipped away during the night in his sleep.

In one of the most-quoted passages of one of the most-performed plays of all time, William Shakespeare said it this way:

> To-morrow, and to-morrow, and to-morrow,
> Creeps in this petty pace from day to day,

To the last syllable of recorded time;
And all our yesterdays have lighted fools
The way to dusty death. Out, out, brief candle!
Life's but a walking shadow, a poor player,
That struts and frets his hour upon the stage,
And then is heard no more; it is a tale
Told by an idiot, full of sound and fury,
Signifying nothing.[2]

It is a howl, frustration and sorrow and loss and fear – what is the meaning of life? I'll tell you – life is a tale told by an idiot! Life is meaningless! Life is too, too short.

Ah, but with Christ, everything has changed. Out of disorder, He teases beauty, out of tragedy, He orchestrates grace. The waiting is charged with purpose, urgency, even. Time *is* short. The song is growing louder. We are going home.

In the meantime, we are undeniably stuck here. 'Under the sun,' says Solomon, cynic of scripture, 'life is really lousy.' As various translations put it, life is meaningless, vanity, vainglory, futility, vapor, emptiness, falsity, smoke. Under the sun there is toil and heartache and devastation and bitter, angry days on end. So how is it that Christ, unflinching, proclaims, 'I came that they may have life and have it abundantly'? Is He speaking of earth-bound souls? Is He mocking me?

Life under the sun is ironically dark, a sinful world bowing to the consequences of our folly. But God does not leave us in darkness; the Word said, '"Let there be light," and there was light.'

---

2. William Shakespeare, *Macbeth*, Act 5, scene 5, 19–28

Light, shining on confusion, suddenly spotlights God's sovereignty, and in a blink, chaos becomes meaningful. Delay becomes opportunity, tragedy is transformed into triumph, and along the way, sniveling, petty humans acquire the dazzling likeness of Christ. But if our perspective can change in an instant, transformation takes a while. And so we wait.

'Patience,' says Oswald Chambers, is critical here, under the sun, where suffering seems to linger forever. It's 'more than endurance. A saint's life is in the hands of God like a bow and arrow in the hands of an archer. God is aiming at something the saint cannot see, and He stretches and strains, and every now and again the saint says – "I cannot stand anymore." God does not heed, He goes on stretching till His purpose is in sight, then He lets fly. Trust yourself in God's hands ... Maintain your relationship to Jesus Christ by the patience of faith. "Though he slay me, yet will I wait for him"(Job 13:15, RV).'[3]

Patience I have in short supply. Perhaps that is exactly why I am asked to wait so often – how else will I learn? He stretches, I strain, the longing becomes so loud a roar in my ears that I cry out. Home! Take me home! And He will; one day, ordinary in the beginning, will by close of day be my homecoming, and looking over my shoulder I will see there is no going back.

---

3. Oswald Chambers, *My Utmost for His Highest*. (Uhrichsville: Barbour Publishing, 1963), 92.

How do we spend the days granted us? How do we live abundantly, fully, richly, deeply satisfied before the sand in the hourglass is gone?

See eternally.
Worship wholeheartedly.
Walk purposefully.
Care passionately.
Give generously.
Hold loosely.
Love deeply.
Stand firm.
Choose light.
Rest.

1: See Eternally

Be Thou my Vision, O Lord of my heart;
Naught be all else to me, save that Thou art.
Thou my best Thought, by day or by night,
Waking or sleeping, Thy presence my light.

Be Thou my Wisdom, and Thou my true Word;
I ever with Thee and Thou with me, Lord;
Thou my great Father, I Thy true son;
Thou in me dwelling, and I with Thee one.

Be Thou my battle Shield, Sword for the fight;
Be Thou my Dignity, Thou my Delight;
Thou my soul's Shelter, Thou my high Tower:
Raise Thou me heavenward, O Power of my power.

Riches I heed not, nor man's empty praise,
Thou mine Inheritance, now and always:
Thou and Thou only, first in my heart,
High King of Heaven, my Treasure Thou art.

High King of Heaven, my victory won,
May I reach Heaven's joys, O bright Heaven's Sun!
Heart of my own heart, whatever befall,
Still be my Vision, O Ruler of all.[1]

He is having a birthday – his eighth. His eyes dance, his feet skip; he is joy itself. 'You are running out of seven-year-old hugs,' I tell him. 'Hurry and give me 1,000 more!' For another year, I won't be nearly as aware as I am today that he is getting older, growing up. For another year, I will fail to notice time slipping through the hourglass. But today I see it. Today the sand is falling fast.

We are very, very small. Consider for a moment that there are over 100 billion stars in the Milky Way alone, and that the Milky Way is only one of billions of galaxies. Try to fathom for a moment the unfathomable distance between each of these perpetually exploding balls of gas – perhaps 20 million million miles between stars[2] – then head out to your front yard and look up. Reel, dizzy, under that spinning disco-ball – do you feel appropriately humble?

---

1. Attributed to Dallan Forgaill, 8th Century (Rob tu mo bhoile, a Comdi cride); translated from ancient Irish to English by Mary E. Byne, in 'Eriú,' *Journal of the School of Irish Learning,* 1905, and versed by Eleanor H. Hull, 1912, alt.

2. Bill Bryson, *A Short History of Nearly Everything.* (New York: Broadway Books, 2003), 27.

Now try to get a grip on how short the last hour of your life was. Whether it was a monumental hour, jammed with exciting or tragic news, or a deadly dull hour spent staring blankly into your refrigerator trying to imagine up some dinner, it was awfully short, one 8,760th of a year. Consider that the technology of your childhood, seemingly so recent, is already obsolete. What kind of telephone did you use? What kind of computer? Remember when you could buy a soda pop for a dime? Probably only forty-five men have lined up in the past 1,000 years before you, fathers of fathers in your family tree. How far back do you remember their names? Four generations? Five? How soon will you be forgotten?

God has set eternity in our hearts, an innate awareness of our smallness and a hunger for all that is lasting. We may sate it temporarily, but temporary is the key word to anything this life can offer. To have an eternal perspective is to take the long view... very long.

The realization that time is ticking has inspired centuries of poets and philosophers, even those who couldn't give a hoot about God. 'Had we but world enough and time,' wrote seventeenth century playboy Andrew Marvel, 'this coyness, lady, were no crime.' Hey, lady, if we were going to live forever, I wouldn't mind a little chastity. But life is short! Let's get busy.

'Carpe diem' – seize the day! shouted the passionate Mr. Keating in *Dead Poets Society*. Find love, live with abandon, pursue your dreams, take a stand. You are not guaranteed tomorrow. Make today count. Even the lost and blind know this truth deep down. (Eccles. 3:11)

Christians, aflame with this understanding, have made the most of short lives, changing the world in remarkable ways with the days they were given. David Brainerd is one. Born some sixty years before the American Revolution, Brainerd was a missionary to the 'heathen Indians' despite the fact that Native Americans and English colonists danced a deadly two-step all around him. Young Brainerd, kicked out of Yale for daring to associate with freewheeling religious types, struggled with despondence and a sickly nature, but determined that his life was not going to be in vain.

I can't even begin to imagine the hardships of a pioneering missionary in the eighteenth century. We are talking DIY house-building with no power tools, kill-and-cook-your-own campfire dinners, sleep on blankets that are not rated for below-freezing temperatures, get your weekly bath in the creek. We are talking hostile warriors with spears and no hesitation to poke you with them, rattlesnakes that share your living space, and no cell phone service. Unfazed, Brainerd forged into this wilderness and began reaching out to the Delaware Indians, who are said to have proclaimed, 'The Great Spirit is with the Paleface!' Lonely enough to sometimes wish he were dead, hungry and depleted, Brainerd persevered for three years, turning down offers to take cushy pastorates along the way. After just a year at his outpost in Crossweeksung, New

Jersey, he had established a 130-member church. He lived hard, he prayed hard, and he died of tuberculosis at just twenty-nine. But his legacy continued; Brainerd's biography inspired the likes of Adoniram Judson, William Carey, and Jim Elliot.

Jim Elliot, of course, is another example. *In The Shadow of the Almighty* has been used to fire up countless college students staring down parallel paths of success and sacrifice. I remember reading it on my parents' front porch, pen in hand, embellishing the pages with exclamation points aplenty. Here were men – Jim Elliot, Nate Saint, Pete Fleming, Ed McCully and Roger Youderian – who lived like meteors, a brilliant flash and they were gone. Because of their furious love and absurd faith (a faith that burned also in the women they left behind), a tribe of Huaorani Indians in Ecuador, astonished, met Christ. 'He is no fool,' said Elliot, 'who gives what he cannot keep to gain what he cannot lose.'

Saint had the same perspective, saying, 'people who do not know the Lord ask why in the world we waste our lives as missionaries. They forget that they too are expending their lives... and when the bubble has burst they will have nothing of eternal significance to show for the years they have wasted.' Giving their lives, they gained the crown of life.

What could I give? What would I gain? The answer to both questions was simple. My life.

I was privileged to know such a person early on; her death rang out like a bell that still reverberates. Since she was twenty-one when she died and I was still in middle school she seemed all grown up. And really, having battled cancer with tenacity and grace, in many ways she was. Her name was Julie Workman. She had been a camp counselor at that same summer camp I'd loved; I watched her laughing, playing with an oversized beach ball, I remember her legs lean and tan, her face lit up in joy. At Julie's funeral, I watched a stream of girls from her college dorm stand to say what impact she had had on their lives. She shone for Christ, she shared His love freely with everyone who crossed her path. In fact, there will be a small crowd of Julie's friends in Heaven, sinners Jesus snatched back from darkness and death, people who will dance on golden streets for eternity. At her funeral, we sang:

> When peace like a river attendeth my way,
> When sorrows like sea billows roll,
> Whatever my lot, Thou hast taught me to say,
> It is well, it is well with my soul.
>
> O Lord, haste the day when my faith shall be sight,
> The clouds be rolled back as a scroll.
> The trump shall resound and the Lord shall descend,
> Even so, it is well with my soul.[3]

Julie made the most of the days she was given, an incredibly rare accomplishment. She took her troubles in her stride, with beautiful faith. What did she fear? She was going home.

***

Moses is not usually remembered as a song writer, but Psalm 90 is attributed to the old law-giver. He

---

3. Horatio G. Spafford, 'It is Well with my Soul', 1873

kicks things off by saying God is old. Really, really old. Older than dirt, in fact. 'Before the mountains were brought forth, or ever you had formed the earth and the world, from everlasting to everlasting you are God.'[4] Before the mountains, You Are. Right now, You Are. Tomorrow, You Are. Or as God had put it to Moses years before: Yahweh. I AM.

Then Moses goes on, 'For a thousand years in your sight are but as yesterday when it is past, or as a watch in the night. You sweep them away as with a flood; they are like a dream, like grass that is renewed in the morning: in the morning it flourishes and is renewed; in the evening it fades and withers... The years of our life are seventy, or even by reason of strength eighty; yet their span is but toil and trouble; they are soon gone, and we fly away.'[5] God is old, but the oldest person in the nursing home only just got started.

Moses does not despair, he takes stock. What shall I do with these short days? How will I find joy? Fortunately, if my life is short, my troubles, too, are light and momentary.

And this realization is a gift: nothing lasts forever, not even deepest sorrow. Suffering may last for a night, but joy comes in the morning. Whatever horror I face is temporary. What conclusion can I draw? Paul says, 'Therefore we do not lose heart. Though outwardly we are wasting away, yet inwardly we are being renewed day by day. For our

---

4. Psalm 90:2
5. Psalm 90:4-6, 10

light and momentary troubles are achieving for us an eternal glory that far outweighs them all. So we fix our eyes not on what is seen, but on what is unseen, since what is seen is temporary, but what is unseen is eternal.'[6]

Though outwardly we are wasting away, it is well with our souls. Suffering is temporary. Suffering is also purposeful, no random accident, but part of the plan of God and achieving weighty glory, glory that puts pain so far in the rear view mirror we can see it no longer. We see 'through a glass darkly' the backside of God's tapestry – a tangle of disorderly threads. But flip it over and you will see the picture He has woven, impossibly beautiful. That dark spot? That was the part that hurt so much.

Even while we struggle with troubles that don't seem very light and momentary, His mercies are new every morning. Inwardly we are renewed day by day, moment by moment if we allow it. We are weary, but He leads us in green pastures, settles us down by quiet waters, restores our souls. He never leaves us nor forsakes us; He quiets us with His love. Though we wade through mighty deep water, the waves shall not consume us. Do not fear.[7]

It's true, my life is a pebble in the vast ocean of the world. But with the days I am given, my little

---

6. 2 Corinthians 4:16-18, (NIV)

7. (light and momentary) 2 Corinthians 4:17, (new every morning) Lamentations 3:22-23, (green pastures, quiet waters, restores our souls) Psalm 23, (inwardly renewed day by day) 2 Corinthians 4:16, (never leaves nor forsakes) Deuteronomy 31:6/Hebrews 13:5, (quiets us with His love) Zephaniah 3:17, (deep water, waves, do not fear) Isaiah 43:2 (paraphrased)

pebble can make a splash. How? Moses, who made a mighty splash, prayed in light of eternity.

> So teach us to number our days
> that we may get a heart of wisdom.
> Return, O Lord! How long?
> Have pity on your servants!
> Satisfy us in the morning with your steadfast love,
> that we may rejoice and be glad all our days.[8]

Jesus, if you will not return this week, teach me to number my days, to order my few hours in order to wring the most good from them. Start me off every morning with a taste of your love, and set the tone for a day that, though short, will matter. Grant me wisdom, an inspired use of minutes. Grant me a life rich in love and joy in the journey.

When I was sixteen, a visiting missionary spoke at our church. Closing out the service, he asked who would be willing to give their lives to missionary service. I sat on the edge of the hard pew, my heart pounding, darting glances at the people praying reverently all around me. Could they hear my thumping heart? Stand up, stand up, coward, I berated myself. You know you ought to! I was young and nerdy. I worried that my clothes weren't cool, my hair didn't cooperate. I didn't want to stand, didn't want to be even more different than I already felt, didn't want to expose myself to ridicule. But what I did want more than anything was to follow Jesus. Some impulse seized my legs, and I hopped to my feet, then sat back down as fast

---

8. Psalm 90:12-14

as I could. Chicken? Yes. But I wanted to make my life count.

Annie Dillard (who sees God in butterfly, tree, tomcat, who could no doubt find grace in a cucumber) put it this way: 'There is always an enormous temptation in all of life to diddle around making itsy-bitsy friends and meals and journeys for itsy-bitsy years on end... I won't have it. The world is wilder than that in all directions, more dangerous and bitter, more extravagant and bright. We are making hay when we should be making whoopee; we are raising tomatoes when we should be raising Cain, or Lazarus.'[9]

I didn't want an itsy-bitsy life. At sixteen, I wanted my little life to ripple long.

At thirty-nine, I am learning a new lesson. If you seek to change the world, you will be satisfied proportionally to your perceived success. You will become a counter, making tally marks: how many 'decisions' were made at the outreach? How many people attended my event? How many people liked my blog, were rescued from human trafficking, liberated from poverty, laid down their weapons, graduated from college? You will weigh your life on one side of the scale against all of the things you hope to change on the other side. Even if you are Billy Graham, or Mother Theresa, you will be found wanting.

---

9. Annie Dillard, *Pilgrim at Tinker Creek.* (New York: HarperPerennial, 1999), 274. As I borrow the quote from Dillard, she borrowed the phrase "itsy-bitsy" from Thomas Merton, who wrote, "There is always a temptation to diddle around in the contemplative life, making itsy-bitsy statues."

But if you seek in your little life one thing: to love the Lord your God with all of your heart, soul, mind, and strength (with a side of loving your neighbor as yourself) well, then you will be satisfied. Period. You will begin, in time, a project that stretches into eternity.

The only ripples that will ripple long begin in my own heart.

***

Having a vision for your life that encompasses all that precedes you and all that will follow is only half of seeing eternally. Equally important is to see the invisible spiritual reality of your world in the here and now. Incredibly, surrounding you this minute there is raging battle on a massive scale. Ahead of you is a destination you cannot yet see, and behind you your struggles and pain have bought blessings you still cannot fathom. You may put your faith in what you can see, hear, taste, touch, smell, or you may put your faith in an invisible, omnipotent God.

One of my favorite Bible stories is tucked away in 2 Kings 6, the brief, matter-of-fact account of an unnamed man, or, as I like to think of it, 'The Curious Incident of the Servant in the Night-time.'

Elisha the prophet has been so faithfully listening to God and relaying His messages to the king of Israel that whichever direction the enemy Syrians turn, the Israelite army has gotten there first and foiled their nefarious plans. In a tantrum of frustration, the Syrian king has decided to annihilate Elisha, the Super Spy, because clearly if your enemy has God on his side, it's a good idea to antagonize him. Accordingly, the Syrian army descends on the city where Elisha is camping out and surrounds it during the night. There is no way out. Elisha, Elisha's servant, the city of Dothan – all are doomed.

> When the servant of the man of God rose early in the morning and went out, behold, an army with horses and chariots was all around the city. And the servant said, 'Alas, my master! What shall we do?' He said, 'Do not be afraid, for those who are with us are more than those who are with them.' Then Elisha prayed and said, 'O Lord, please open his eyes that he may see.' So the Lord opened the eyes of the young man, and he saw, and behold, the mountain was full of horses and chariots of fire all around Elisha. And when the Syrians came down against him, Elisha prayed to the Lord and said, 'Please strike this people with blindness.' So he struck them with blindness in accordance with the prayer of Elisha.[10]

Despite the obvious impossibility of escape, Elisha, His servant, and the people of Dothan did escape. What seemed obvious to Elisha's servant was based squarely on his five senses, but the unseen reality of the situation painted a different picture. Ultimately, those with eyes to see won the day, and those who lost faltered because of blindness. True then, true now: vision is key to victory.

---

10. 2 Kings 6:15-18

This theme of the invisible runs through the Bible, a tantalizing mystery. In Daniel, a strange account: Daniel, humble man of prayer, receives a vision in which a man 'like lightning' speaks to him.

> Then he said to me, 'Fear not, Daniel, for from the first day that you set your heart to understand and humbled yourself before your God, your words have been heard, and I have come because of your words. The prince of the kingdom of Persia withstood me twenty-one days, but Michael, one of the chief princes, came to help me, for I was left there with the kings of Persia, and came to make you understand what is to happen to your people in the latter days. For the vision is for days yet to come.'[11]

Come again? Daniel, man of earth, has been praying on scabby knees on a dusty floor, unaware that his prayer has triggered some kind of heavenly battle. As he waits (that agonizing waiting), angels and demons wrestle, unseen, above his head. Of course, Daniel, not knowing of this swashbuckling drama, may either continue to pour out his heart before the Lord, or give up and go home in a fit of despair. How long, O Lord, to sing this song? But Daniel, man of prayer, plows on. The angels win, the prayer is answered, the waiting is finally over.

In the waiting, do you lose heart? God is not dead, nor does He sleep. The hiddenness of God does not indicate His absence, His apathy, or even His inaction, just our own blindness. We can't see

---

11. Daniel 10:12-14

God or His host of angels any more than we can see electrons whirling around in our fingertip. That doesn't mean God isn't there.

Infants enter the world without the ability to trust the invisible. Peek-a-boo is startling to a baby because the baby cannot fathom that Dad, having disappeared, is still in the building. Psychologists say that developing a sense of 'object permanence' is one of the first milestones of an infant's cognitive growth. So it is for the born again. Christ, the Rock, must be to us a permanent object, or we are forever stunted, spiritual babies, subject to panic. Where is He? I can't see Him! I have been waiting five whole minutes!

In the waiting, faith.

'Now faith is the assurance of things hoped for, the conviction of things not seen.'[12] Faith is unnecessary when visual evidence is in supply. Should God condescend to give you a roadmap of His plans, you can hang your faith on a hook and rely on divine GPS. In the meantime, faith is the choice of a blind man to trust another's eyes, to trust enough to run.

While we wait, heaven, too, is waiting. In Hebrews, we read that we are surrounded by a great cloud of witnesses, believers gone before us, cheering us on. Run, therefore, even when you are afraid and blind. The finish line is near. The stands are packed, the cheering is a roar. The reward is sweet.

'If I weep,' sang Rich Mullins, 'let it be as a man who is longing for his home.' Are you homesick? What a home you have to look forward to.

---

12. Hebrews 11:1

In Isaiah, Ezekiel, and Revelation we are treated to bizarre descriptions of heaven, relayed by people powerless to articulate what they have been privileged to see. No time traveling involved, mind you – what they glimpsed of heaven was there all along, is there even now, out of sight. The veil briefly lifted, the vision cleared, and hey ho! More than meets the eye. A crystal-clear sea, a city gleaming like jewels, the river of life overhung with orchards straight from Eden... above all, seated high on a throne, the King of Kings, so magnificent in power and glory that even the seraphim cover their eyes, overcome with perpetual awe. This is your home. Seeing eternally means seeing with eyes of faith what we cannot yet see with eyes brown, blue, or green, and translating that faith into footsteps.

C.S. Lewis wrote eloquently about eternal perspective, delighting generations of children with stories of an unseen kingdom. While Peter, Susan, Edmund and Lucy may appear to be ordinary children in London, they are in fact kings and queens of Narnia. Yet as Lewis unpacked in his nonfiction, he perceived that most Christians do not live like citizens of heaven, children of the King. As he wrote in *Weight of Glory,* 'We are half-hearted creatures, fooling about with drink and sex and ambition when infinite joy is offered us, like an ignorant child who wants to go on making mud pies in a slum because he cannot imagine what is meant by the offer of a holiday at the sea. We are far too easily pleased.'[13]

---

13. C.S. Lewis, *The Weight of Glory*. (New York: HarperCollins, 2001), 26.

What would it mean to put aside the mud pies and seize infinite joy? To begin to ignore the sensory signals bombarding us and tune in to invisible reality? If indeed that thing of utmost importance to me is entirely insignificant, a mud pie in light of eternity, if in fact my life is ephemeral as vapor, then what is worthwhile?

To have an abundant life, rich and full, means seeing the shortness of the day and seizing it, living the bucket list before the sun sets. It requires the quick gulp and the leaping blind, discarding what is heavy and worthless, investing in eternal things, counting as precious the gifts as they come and holding them loose because they will soon be gone.

To live life to the full means to 'give what you cannot keep to gain what you cannot lose.' What will you trade? A life of comfort and convenience for a life of challenge and reward? A heavy burden you were never meant to bear for Jesus' yoke, easy and light?

Sara Groves, singer and poet, penned a gorgeous rewrite of 'When the Saints Go Marching In'[14]. She sings about the potentially overwhelming burden of compassion in a broken world. When we see children starving or humans trafficked or even the struggles of friends in bad marriages, how can we possibly stand up under the load of it all? Thankfully, we don't have to. Jesus' call to us invites us into challenge, yes, but relieves us of

---

14. Sara Groves, 'When the Saints' from the album *Tell Me What You Know* (INO Records, 2007).

burdensome worry. He's got this! Groves sings that when she considers those who have gone before, those who have faithfully, joyfully served Christ – not saving the world, but shining in their own little corner of it – she gains courage. From Paul and Silas to modern missionary heroes, the saints who go marching ahead of us lend us perspective. As Groves says, 'I want to be one of them.'

When I'm 'weary and overwrought,' worn down by life under the sun, I can remember that I am not of this world; I am a child of the King, living for an invisible Kingdom. The trade, the choice to forsake what is petty and meaningless (and with it the cumbersome stress that drags us down) and chase after what is hard, but good, is what will rescue me. It is the giving up of rights, the counting it all as joy to suffer with Jesus. The saints march in, glorious, on the profit of that trade. Will we? Lay it all down, and the things of earth will grow strangely dim, the unholy clamor will recede into the background, all will fall into perspective.

2: Worship Wholeheartedly

Choosing one thing over another doesn't necessarily mean we love the thing we choose. If given the choice to eat spinach or broccoli, you may choose broccoli. It may only mean you don't want to eat spinach. Heaven is not for people who want to skip Hell. Heaven is reserved for those who love Jesus, who have been rescued by Him and who long to praise Him. If someone doesn't have much use for praising Him now, it's foolish to think they're ready for Heaven.

– Matt Chandler,
Creature of the Word: The Jesus-Centered Church[1]

---

1. Matt Chandler and Eric Geiger, *Creature of the Word: The Jesus-Centered Church*. (Nashville: B & H Publishing Group, 2012), 40.

So we're all sojourners, traveling home. And when you're traveling, really only one thing is absolutely important.

We were headed to Florida to meet up with old friends: my husband, my toddler, my newborn baby girl. After a year or so living in frozen Wisconsin, I was uber-excited to be headed to the land of perpetual sunshine. (Also slightly paranoid that Little Guy would drown). We'd packed sunscreen and bathing suits, flip flops and toothpaste, enough new baby gear to fill a small shopping mall. The cheapest flight left from Madison, two hours from our home, and as we zipped down the highway into Dane County, we breathed a little easier. The packing was done, the details were in place, it was time to fly off on our little vacation. Close to the airport, I pulled out my purse. Might as well be ready for curbside check-in, save the drama of two babies in a long line. Alas, as I dug through my wallet I saw with a shock – no driver's license.

It was 2003, not long after 9/11. Airport security guards had long passed the days of trusting passengers. There was no way they were letting me on that plane.

What do you do? If we went back for it, we'd all miss the plane. All that money! No, the only thing to do was to put the rest of the family on their flight, wave goodbye, and buy a new ticket, meet them tomorrow. How in the world did I forget my license?

By some miracle, though, I made it on that flight. The airline attendant, struck with compassion, surveyed my Sam's Club card (photo ID), library card (municipal ID), teary eyes, and waved me through. What??

You can buy diapers at your destination. You can even buy a whole week's worth of clothes. But one thing you can't buy is an out-of-state driver's license. We asked a friend to break in to our house, find the ID, Fed-Ex it to Florida (just in case the next airline attendant didn't like my Sam's Club card). I wouldn't try it my way if I were you.

One thing.

In the old movie *City Slickers*, a jaded New Yorker named Mitch surveys his life and finds it lacking. Is this all there is? Reluctantly, Mitch embarks on an 'adventure vacation,' an opportunity to wrangle cattle, ride horses, and camp in wild west wilderness. Mitch and his buddies nurse their saddle sores around campfires at night and discuss at some length their dissatisfaction, a persistent sense that they'd somehow missed out on the best life. Across the miles of trails, they seek some deeper, more mystical truth. Mitch in particular is captivated by a Hollywood-vague bit of advice proffered by the surly cowboy Curly: the answer to all his problems is 'one thing.' Curly refuses to expound upon this bit of deep wisdom, and Mitch is left to ponder: what is the one thing?

In both the Old and New Testaments, we are advised, not lightly, to seek 'one thing.' David puts it like this in Psalm 27:4, 'One thing have I asked of the Lord, that will I seek after: that I may dwell in the house of the Lord all the days of my life, to gaze upon the beauty of the Lord and to inquire in his temple.'

In all the days of our earth-bound lives, there is only one thing essential to the journey, one thing which is the solution to all our woes, one thing capable of bringing light, clarity, joy, purpose or meaning into our existence. God alone is not bound to the sour sadness of the fall. He is above, beyond, and outside this sin-sick planet, not stuck 'under the sun' with us. He is unstained, perfect in love and power. Gazing upon the beauty of the Lord is the only relief from seeing the squalor all around. Dwelling in His presence is our ticket to escaping mud pies and slums.

It is a bit difficult to keep one's eyes focused on the invisible, however. Life is complicated and messy down here at ground zero. How can I pause to worship Jesus when I am so darn busy? Consider the story of Mary and Martha from Luke 10:38-42.

> As they continued their travel, Jesus entered a village. A woman by the name of Martha welcomed him and made him feel quite at home. She had a sister, Mary, who sat before the Master, hanging on every word he said. But Martha was pulled away by all she had to do in the kitchen. Later, she stepped in, interrupting them. 'Master, don't you care that my sister has abandoned the kitchen to me? Tell her to lend me a hand.'
>
> The Master said, 'Martha, dear Martha, you're fussing far too much and getting yourself worked up over nothing. One thing only is essential, and Mary has chosen it—it's the main course, and won't be taken from her.' (MSG)

One thing – essential, important, delicious, best. The 'one thing' is really one person, Jesus. Higher and more important than any to-do list, any worry, that one Other thing that's been on your mind all week. More important, in Martha's case, than the urgency of feeding a crowd of who's-whos descending on her home, more important, even, than her service for Jesus, was the Word Himself. Who knows what words He spoke in that living room, what word He might have longed to speak to Martha, if only she'd had time to listen?

The highest, best, and really the only key to an abundant life, rich and full, is a life of whole-hearted worship. To live at the feet of the Savior, to dwell in the tabernacle of the Almighty, here is peace! Here is promised rest. As the old carol puts it,

> O ye beneath life's crushing load,
> Whose forms are bending low,
> Who toil along the climbing way
> With painful steps and slow;
> Look now, for glad and golden hours
> Come swiftly on the wing;
> Oh, rest beside the weary road
> And hear the angels sing.

It Came Upon a Midnight Clear
Edmund Sears, 1849

Life got you down? Rest at the scarred feet, gaze upon the lovely, homely face, and hear His particular words for you. Here is the only rest to be had under the sun.

I live with my family in a somewhat impoverished sector of the sprawling Denver metro area. In 1995, I spent a summer here, my first summer immersed in inner-city life, inner-city ministry. I lived with seventeen other college students on old mattresses in the dusty back rooms of an urban church, housed in what had been a supermarket before neighborhood violence and an awful murder shut the store down completely. The words for the church in Pergamum might have been for this church: 'I know where you live – where Satan has his throne.' For weeks, I passed out animal crackers to barefooted immigrant children, laughed with gang-banger teens, fed homeless, toothy old men, and prayed brazenly against the devil. I fell completely in love with the people, with the city, with the thrill of serving Christ.

But there is a downside to inner-city ministry, one I didn't entirely grasp that first summer, something I have had to swallow as a bitter pill in the years since. In order to love the least of these, you must live among them, on mean streets, in dirty alleys. The blocks without fathers become your blocks, the neighbors with violent tempers become your neighbors, the filth in the gutters blows into your yard. And if you live in a large, high-traffic city, you will know, too, that it is hard to see the stars for the street lights.

I remember going with our intrepid little collegiate group up into the mountains after weeks in the city. At night, I was transfixed to see again the stars. The entire Milky Way, glorious across a pitch-black sky, unobscured by high rises and police lights, was truly amazing – literally breath-taking; the flash of meteorites made me gasp.

The beauty of Christ is easily obscured by the flashing lights of a godless world. It takes intentionality to find a quiet place to see. And without seeing, without peering, studying, meditating, it is all too easy to 'lose your first love.' And that is where every philandering husband first goes astray – 'it doesn't hurt to look, does it?'

Worship, boiled down, is love, quite different qualitatively from respect, or loyalty. Love usually begins with emotion but is sustained by choice, nurtured by tenderness and attention, and carefully guarded. But many, offering numb obedience, call it love, equating a tow-the-line mentality with devotion. It is true that God desires obedience ('to obey is better than sacrifice,' according to 1 Sam. 15:22), but also clear that He desires deeply our very hearts.

> 'Love me with all your heart' – Based on Deuteronomy 6:5; 13:3; 30:6, Matthew 22:37, Mark 12:30-33, Luke 10:27

> 'Serve me with all your heart' – Based on Deuteronomy 10:12; 11:13, Joshua 22:5, 1 Samuel 12:20-24

> 'Trust me with all your heart' – Proverbs 3:5

> 'Seek me with all your heart' – Based on Deuteronomy 4:29, Psalm 119:2; Psalm 119:10, Jeremiah 29:13

> 'Praise me with all your heart' – Based on Psalm 9:1; Psalm 86:12; Psalm 138:1

'Follow me with all your heart' – Based on
1 Kings 14:8

And finally, the right context for obedience,
'Obey me with all your heart' – Based on
Deuteronomy 30:2-10; Psalm 119:34

Furthermore, we are instructed to have a heart
that is soft toward God (1 Sam. 6:6, Ps. 95:8,
Prov. 28:14), pounds for God (Song 5:4), is
fully devoted (1 Kings 11:4, 1 Kings 15:3), is
stirred (Ps. 45:1), steadfast (Ps. 57:7, Ps. 108:1,
Ps. 112:7), secure (Ps. 112:8), and undivided
(Ps. 86:11, Ezek. 11:19). We are 'above all else' to
guard our hearts (Prov. 4:23), to keep our hearts
pure (Ps. 73:13, Prov. 20:9, Prov. 22:11, Matt. 5:8,
2 Tim. 2:22) , to rend our hearts (Joel 2:13), to be
glad and rejoice with all our hearts (Zeph. 3:14),
and if we have strayed, to return to Him with all our
hearts (1 Sam. 7:3, Jer. 3:10, Jer. 24:7, Joel 2:12),
to treasure His word in our hearts (Deut. 11:18,
Ps. 119:11), and to cultivate sincerity of heart
(Eph. 6:5, Heb. 10:22, 1 Pet. 1:22).

An abundant life, then, is a life lit by love,
a life lived fully from the heart. It is glimpsed for
a moment by anyone who's ever been swept off
their feet, finding themselves all astonishment at
the sudden, unprecedented surge of feeling that
makes the rest of their workaday world irrelevant.
It is the kind of life experienced through peaks
and valleys, heartbreak and delight, for a long
and glad century by all who truly learn to love
Christ.

Love tumbles out of a full heart, spilling onto anyone close by. It is the purest form of worship, a joyful, trusting devotion. Love is inherently humble, springing up into happy service and ungrudging obedience. Think of the dog in Pixar's *Up* – 'You are my master and I love you!'

The passage of 1 Timothy 1:12 carries a sense of this attitude: 'I thank him who has given me strength, Christ Jesus our Lord, because he judged me faithful, appointing me to his service...' Who, me? Paul is the eager kindergartner, wishing above all to please the teacher. Ooh, me, me, pick me! I want to pass out the crayons! I want to hand out the books. Worship is the fuel for service.

Sometimes I come across people with the mindset that service for God, missionary service at least, is some kind of elite calling. My husband and I have been paraded around like heroes because of our decision to work for God full-time. Frankly, it is hard for me to imagine spending a lifetime in any other service. Serve a corporation? It brings Ecclesiastes to mind again, that 'toilsome labor under the sun.' Seems to me that serving God through working in a money-making organization would be a special call, the extraordinary and rare life of a double agent: salesman by trade, disciple in disguise. But by all means, God wired each individual uniquely, and the careful study of what brings me greatest joy also leads to the discovery of what I think He made me uniquely to do. So a runner might say that when he runs, he feels God's good pleasure. My friend Angela feels His pleasure in accounting. Life is full of mysteries.

Here's the caution: let your life flow from the love of God, live in a way that enhances your love of God, or wither.

To voluntarily spend a life chained to a cubicle doing a job you disdain is to set yourself up for a halfhearted life. I don't say it is impossible to please God under the circumstances, but you've definitely made it more difficult to live every day in joyful obedience, from the heart. My own heart has a tendency to shrivel up when my gifts are untapped, my talents unexplored, and my passions dormant. Pay attention! If your heart is drying up, this is an unacceptable state of affairs. Joyless, discontented, frustrated, resigned misery is not God-honoring; isn't the fruit of the Spirit love, joy, peace? Either learn to give thanks where you are – real thanksgiving, sincere and heartfelt – learn to give glory to God through excellence and patience, seek in your job opportunities to do eternal things every day (love, give, share Christ), or, if still the job is poisonous to your heart, dare to kick free of its entanglement and start over.

'No one can serve two masters, for either he will hate the one and love the other, or he will be devoted to one and despise the other. You cannot serve God and money. Therefore I tell you, do not be anxious about your life, what you will eat or what you will drink, nor about your body, what you will put on. Is not life more than food, and the body more than clothing? Look at the birds of the air; they neither sow nor reap nor gather into barns, and yet your heavenly Father feeds them. Are you not of more value than they?'[2] If you can't worship God wholeheartedly in your career, then you need a new boss, and the heck with your comfortable salary.

***

A heart full of worship leaps at the opportunity to worship through obedience, whatever strange requirements God makes. Springing from that sense of devotion, David Livingstone said: 'Forbid that we should ever consider the holding of a commission from the King of Kings a sacrifice, so long as other men esteem the service of an earthly government as an honor. I am a missionary, heart and soul. God Himself had an only Son, and He was a missionary and a physician. A poor, poor imitation I am, or wish to be, but in this service I hope to live. In it I wish to die. I still prefer poverty and missions service to riches and ease. This is my choice.' He speaks of service, but it is the wholehearted kind, a by-product of love. It is the worship of hands and feet.

Wholehearted worship is a gift that we give God, one of the only gifts we are indeed able to give. It delights God, who Himself is never shy to lavish on His loving children incredible gifts. The fact of the matter is that our love is but a 'poor, poor imitation' of His own: His love is patient, kind, never failing. Our lives are made rich and full by the ridiculous outpouring of God's love toward us. He calls out to us,

> 'The Lord your God is with you, he is mighty to save. He will take great delight in you, he will

---

2.   Matthew 6:24-26

quiet you with his love, he will rejoice over you with singing. How wide and long and high and deep is the love of Christ, this love that surpasses knowledge? Many rivers cannot quench love, rivers cannot wash it away. As a bridegroom rejoices over his bride, so will your God rejoice over you.

'Fear not, for I have redeemed you, I have summoned you by name, you are mine. I will not forget you. See, I have engraved you on the palms of my hands. I have loved you with an everlasting love; I have drawn you with loving-kindness. Never will I leave you, never will I forsake you.'[3]

'We love him because he first loved us' (1 John 4:19), miracle of miracles, and we are blown away. We love Him back with unstinting love, not because we are oh-so-holy, but because, glimpsing His love, we can't help it. Out pours our delight, and in response, He pours out blessings heaped up, pressed down, running over (Luke 6:38). Like children at Christmas, we are delighted. We worship.

***

Experimentally, I wrote down a list of the commands found in Psalm 37. What would it be like to follow them faithfully for a season? It is a basic recipe for abundant life: Don't fret, trust, dwell, do good, *delight*, commit, be still, wait, don't fret. Not overly burdensome. Not especially elitist. Simple, freeing,

---

3. Adapted from the following verses: Zephaniah 3:17, Ephesians 3:18, Song of Songs 8:7, Isaiah 62:5, Isaiah 43:1, Isaiah 49:16, Jeremiah 31:3, Hebrews 13:5

worshipful. And the Lord, for His part, gives so freely back. For every command, a promise: don't fret – He will vanquish evil. Trust – you will enjoy safe pasture. *Delight yourself in the Lord, and He will give you the desires of your heart.* It is a call to worship, and the emotional response it evokes is ahhhhh.

It's a bit tricky these days to point out the blessings involved in following Jesus without sounding a parrot of the prosperity gospel. Give to God, and He'll give to you! Well, true. And sometimes, quite spectacular. But it is usually not in blank checks. Our children still get sick, our bills still stuff the mailbox. There are long seasons of drought, and often we are assailed by doubt and confusion. But sometimes I am so shy of sounding like a purple-sunglasses-white-suit TV preacher that I don't acknowledge the shocking gifts of God lavished on a regular Joe with childlike faith.

But He does give – gives joy, freedom, little miracles of good health and parking spaces, happy coincidences and sheer beauty. For a homesick soul, God's good gifts are like care packages for a lonely college freshman far from her hometown. Unwrap them, and it's – hey, chocolate chip cookies! Letter of love from dear old Dad! When you take delight in the Lord, you begin to see, spread out before you, a thousand ways He's anticipated, shaped, and met the desires of your heart in ways big and small.

Annie Dillard tells a beautiful story to set the stage for her observant meditations in *Pilgrim at Tinker Creek*. As a child in Pittsburgh, Dillard delighted in hiding pennies around the neighborhood for strangers to discover. So vividly she sets the scene that I feel I can see her crouching behind a tree, little grubby hand clamped over her mouth to stop from laughing. Her hiding skills were perhaps less than stellar since she took pains to draw arrows to these treasures, marking some, as she says, 'SURPRISE AHEAD or MONEY THIS WAY.' But her desire to delight lucky passersby looks a lot like God's. And we, the unsuspecting, lucky strangers, have quite an opportunity. Dillard writes,

> I've been thinking about seeing. There are lots of things to see, unwrapped gifts and free surprises. The world is fairly studded and strewn with pennies cast broadside from a generous hand. But – and this is the point – who gets excited by a mere penny? If you follow one arrow, if you crouch motionless on a bank to watch a tremulous ripple thrill on the water and are rewarded by the sight of a muskrat kit paddling from its den, will you count that sight a chip of copper only, and go your rueful way? It is dire poverty indeed when a man is so malnourished and fatigued that he won't stoop to pick up a penny. But if you cultivate a healthy poverty and simplicity, so that finding a penny will literally make your day, then, since the world is in fact planted in pennies, you have with your poverty bought a lifetime of days. It is that simple.[4]

A whole universe, planted in pennies, unbridled extravagance of Love... God loving us so easily that

---

4.   Annie Dillard, *Pilgrim at Tinker Creek.* (New York: HarperCollins, 1998) 16-17.

we cannot help but worship... It is a never-ending cycle, or would be, if we weren't so easily distracted.

One thing: to sit at the feet of Love, amazed, delighted, entranced. This is the one thing that can rescue a humdrum life and set it humming.

3: Walk Purposefully

If you want to identify me, ask me not where I live, or what I like to eat, or how I comb my hair, but ask me what I am living for, in detail, ask me what I think is keeping me from living fully for the thing I want to live for.

My Argument with the Gestapo, Thomas Merton[1]

I must keep alive in myself the desire for my true country, which I shall not find till after death; I must never let it get snowed under or turned aside; I must make it the main object of life to

---

1.   *My Argument with the Gestapo* by Thomas Merton. (New York: New Directions, 1975), 160-1

*press on to that other country and to help others
do the same.*
Mere Christianity, C.S. Lewis[2]

When I was in about seventh grade, our family joined a new swimming pool, and my mother persuaded me to try the tennis team. None of my friends had played much tennis, so she reasoned I wouldn't be too far behind. I could learn a new sport, get some exercise, some sun, make some friends. (At this point in the story you should already be shaking your head sadly, muttering sympathy for my little seventh-grade-self and her tennis dream. If you have met me, you might actually have fallen from whatever perch you were sitting on and found yourself now rolling on the floor in uncontrollable, gasping laughter. Yeah, me and sports. It's that bad.)

The hapless tennis instructor, confronted with my incredible ability to send balls flying willy-nilly over the fence and baffled by my lost-in-space tendency to not notice when someone was hitting the ball to me, soon had a brilliant solution to my purpose on the team. 'Kate,' she said eagerly (after maybe one lesson), 'you can be *the ball girl.*' Well, it made her happy, but I didn't want to be the ball girl. She might as well have given me a name tag that said, 'Hello, my name is incompetent.' That was the end of my participation on the Friendly Pool Tennis Team.

---

2. *Mere Christianity* (New York: The MacMillan Company, 1952), 106.

Purpose, or the lack of it, is a game-changer. Ask a clever elementary school teacher what to do with a naughty kid who's really, really bored. You give him purpose. Here, Jack, you can be in charge of feeding the class turtle! Now Jack has a job, his presence there has new meaning, and Jack might just start having good days... at least sometimes.

Perhaps your purpose is painfully unclear. Maybe you feel stuck, constrained by circumstances beyond your control. How many people in that situation would be depressed? Hopeless? But if you discover purpose, that in fact God put you where you are for a reason, your life might just be transformed in amazing ways.

Joni Eareckson Tada was a popular, vibrant teenager when she dove into Chesapeake Bay and hit her head, becoming a quadriplegic. Never again would she ride horses, swim, try out for the tennis team. But that girl found some serious purpose. Someone put a paintbrush in her mouth and she rediscovered her talent and passion for painting beautiful pictures – with her teeth! Not only that, she had a message to share, an urgent, compelling, beautiful message. She began to write books, took up public speaking. Joni Eareckson Tada has changed many people's lives as a direct result of her accident and her faithfulness to God under the circumstances.

Or take a look at the Ten Boom sisters. Corrie and Betsy's undercover ministry of helping Jews escape from the Nazis was cruelly cut short when they themselves were caught and sent to a concentration camp. What good could possibly come of that? God, were you asleep at the wheel? But it was there, in a flea-infested prison, that Corrie's and Betsy's lives really began to shine. There in the darkness they found purpose, and shared the love of Christ with many desperate and dying people. When Corrie made it out alive (Betsy did not), she brought a message of hope and forgiveness to the world.

While God does not always transform our context, He is often willing to gloriously redeem it. God clearly made Joni, Corrie, and Betsy with a purpose in mind – not perhaps the path they might have chosen, but one of triumph and (unexpectedly) joy. What about you?

There are many Christians, grateful for salvation, who occasionally wonder what to do with the 80-90 years they've been given, but mostly go about their weeks oblivious. On Monday they pay the water bill. On Tuesday they pop in on the early bird special at Luigi's Pizza. On Sunday, they might go to church.

It won't do to love God ever-so-much on Sundays but forget Him six days a week. Wholehearted worship can't be turned on and off like a light switch; if it is real it must be practiced.

***

Maddening, the book of James can be, seeming to topple all of our lofty grace-alone theology in a frenzy of works, but there you have it: faith without works is dead. Or, in more detail: 'But be doers of the word, and not hearers only, deceiving yourselves. For if anyone is a hearer of the word and not a doer, he is like a man who looks intently at his natural face in a mirror. For he looks at himself and goes away and at once forgets what he was like. But the one who looks into the perfect law, the law of liberty, and perseveres, being no hearer who forgets but a doer who acts, he will be blessed in his doing' (James 1:22-25).

There is something to be said for doing something. And indeed, it is a freeing something we are meant to do: follow 'the law of liberty.' The Pharisees, with their 999 rules, can go jump in a lake. We've just got two: love God, love your neighbor. As the psalmist says, 'The lines have fallen for me in pleasant places; indeed, I have a beautiful inheritance' (Ps. 16:6).

Here are the boundary lines; do not cross. Stay in your appointed pasture. Jesus said the yoke is easy, the burden is light, but it is, after all, a yoke. There is an analogy here, and we are the cattle in question.

Part, I think, of living abundantly comes from the doing. It is a faith expressed in works, a belief lived out seven days a week, a following with abandon our Master into uncharted territory, cattle herded where He will lead. We are asked very explicitly to walk with Christ, to cling to Him when we can see only the step immediately in front of us. If we resist ('no, you go on ahead, Lord, I'll just sit a spell'), we obviously fall out of step with Him, drift into aimlessness, fall away. But if we walk with

Him, He suffuses our lives with purpose. Purpose colors everything, a bank of stained glass windows filling the sanctuary with sapphire, emerald, ruby. God defines for us the reason for our lives, giving meaning to our long days and suffering nights.

So what is our purpose? The Westminster Catechism has it this way: 'The chief end of man is to glorify God and enjoy Him forever.' John Piper would tweak it: 'The chief end of man is to glorify God by enjoying Him forever.'[3] In other words, your purpose is not to live a self-centered life with salvation as your just reward. Nor is it a life of mindless obedience void of laughter. Your very reason for being here on Earth is to enjoy God and reflect Him powerfully, uniquely, in a particular way that only you can. It begins here, in the muck of Earth, and continues forever, an eternity of joy in Christ.

***

This working, this walking, is no mild-mannered day job. It is espionage, intrigue, battle, guts.

Imagine you're the appointed American ambassador to a fascinating Asian nation. The two countries teeter on the brink of war, the very air is charged with tension. You must work patiently, carefully behind the scenes to prevent catastrophe. But their customary afternoon nap and tea is so charming! There are delicacies you long to sample, markets to explore, beaches to visit. After a few lazy

---

3.   John Piper. *Desiring God* (Colorado Springs: Multnomah, 2011), 18.

months, you renounce your citizenship, adopt this foreign land as your home. Your mission is abandoned, forgotten, cast aside.

This is the sad story of any Christ-follower who ceases to follow.

We are Christ's ambassadors, Paul explains in 2 Corinthians, living in constant danger of death. We are aliens and strangers, says Peter, sojourners far from home.[4] How could we forget our call? And really, what could be more invigorating than to be entrusted with a critical mission, the fate of the world in the balance?

Is that actually our situation, or have I overstated my case? Paul writes, 'How then will they call on him in whom they have not believed? And how are they to believe in him of whom they have never heard? And how are they to hear without someone preaching? And how are they to preach unless they are sent? As it is written, "How beautiful are the feet of those who preach the good news!"' (Rom. 10:14-15) We are privileged to be on the good-news committee, people of the pedicure. Without needing us, God nevertheless chooses us to participate in His save-the-world mission, rescuing souls who've hopelessly lost their way.

It's not about checking off my evangelism quota for the week, either. Sharing Christ in a God-glorifying way is just relishing Him... in public. Like standing around the free fudge samples at Costco and raving, 'This is the most delicious stuff you

---

4.   1 Peter 2:11

ever put in your mouth! Oh my gosh, you have to try it!' If you really love Him, you're going to talk about Him. You can't help it.

There is something that seems awfully tacky about evangelism, especially if you perceive a division of teams in Christianity: the fundamentalist (doing) team, the open-minded (thinking) team. Hip young Christians shun the fundies like a plague. (The very idea of hip young Christians is problematic, though – there is nothing sexy about humility.) The fundies revile the liberalism of the young'uns. This division is demonic. Pick sides, do you want to use your brains or your feet? If Satan can play the one against the other, he has brilliantly won a battle. Put a megaphone in the hand of the person least reasoned and he has branded us all idiots. Atrophy the muscles of the person most mindful and he has forestalled a movement.

But if, brain working, feet moving, we seek to discover where God is at work, where our unique personality and skills might come into play, what, indeed, our personal mission is in the greater scheme of God's save-the-world plan, well, then our purpose becomes crystal clear. 'For we are his workmanship, created in Christ Jesus for good works, which God prepared beforehand, that we should walk in them.' (Eph. 2:10) I was created with a mission in mind.

Your purpose (to glorify God by enjoying Him forever) and your personal mission (the who/what/ when/where/how of it) jointly take into account your gifts, your talents, your passions, and your context. It wouldn't make very much sense for God to call Joni Eareckson Tada to work with persecuted Jews in a Nazi concentration camp, or for Corrie ten Boom to paint with her mouth or indeed for me, the worst ball girl in the world, to attempt to shine for Christ on the courts at Wimbledon. It would be ludicrous to chuck aside the things you are passionate about or good at and try to serve God in some way you deem more worthy; the God who made you love math or singing or research made you that way with some forethought. Brother Lawrence scrubbed dishes in a monastery, Dorothy Sayers wrote witty mysteries, Elisabeth Elliot went to Ecuador. Each did what he or she was called to do.

Likewise, it wouldn't be wise to disregard your context geographically or historically.

If you are reading this, I can confidently make a few assumptions about your context. You read Christian books in English in your free time. You must not be starving, homeless, destitute, or otherwise in survival mode. You must be educated (at least literate), and this must have happened in an affluent, English-speaking world. Is this pertinent to your purpose and mission? Did God place you here intentionally?

Consider that around the world, the vast majority of pastors (pastors!) do not have in their native language more than a handful of commentaries, theological books, or the training and resources you could acquire in one afternoon on the Internet. Consider that there are thousands of people groups with no Bible at all in their mother tongue. Consider that you have more money at your disposal than 95 per cent of the human beings on the planet if you live at some sort of permanent address and have a couple of cars parked out front. While millions of people struggle just to feed their babies, you can happily sip a latte and read this book for fun. When for thousands of years, a 100-mile trip was almost beyond imagination, you can zip around the globe in a day, with in-flight entertainment and pretzels. You have *opportunity*.

Now stack it up. I am good at _____. I like to _____. I could both enjoy God and glorify Him by _____ in such-and-such a place. Who needs what I have? Who would be blessed by what I can do? Where you see the best intersection of your neighbor's need and your own abilities might be a good place to start. So for example, there may very well be a huge need for a Bible translation in Papua New Guinea, but here you are with a special-needs kid who relies on the nearby hospital in Oklahoma City (and you're really more of a gourmet chef than a linguist). Hmm, what to do? When you think about it, there is a significant homeless population in Oklahoma City and a soup kitchen that could use an upgrade from pork and beans. Voila! Their need plus your gifting equals step one. (While you're at it, maybe sending a tithe of your fabulous restaurant's profits to a New Guinea translation team might be warranted.)

Your purpose and mission on a daily, lived-in basis, might be as simple as inviting your boss's family over for supper once in a while and being unashamed of the gospel. It might be as radical as adopting an orphan or selling all you have and moving to New Guinea. But it's your heart that counts – are you doing what you do because you love and treasure Jesus above all?

As Mae West famously quipped, 'You only live once, but if you do it right, once is enough.' Take your short life and make it count.

Jesus, in thirty-three years, seemed not to accomplish very much. His little band of followers was terrifically ordinary, despised by the world, and short on courage. Jesus Himself wrote no books and began no rebellion. No doubt the Pharisees and the Romans both were fairly smug to get Jesus out of the picture. *Well, that's over.* Of course, they underestimated Him a tad. One life, fully lived, epic. You protest that Jesus had an edge, being God and all. True. But He left His mission in the hands of those ragtag followers, eleven scaredy-cat fishermen and a handful of ostracized women. A team about the size of a pair of small groups in a suburban church changed the world. What's your small group done lately?

That was snarky; I apologize. But there is unquestionably a disconnect between the lifestyle of the Acts 4 church and the post-modern western congregation. The early church keenly felt its life-or-death, do-or-die situation. To follow Christ was downright dangerous, and not to be done lightly. As it has been for every persecuted generation since, there was a heightened sense of urgency linked with the call to Christ. So when the believers in Acts 4 share all that they have, they are not attempting to set up a communist nation, they are circling the wagons. They pray not in regularly scheduled, reserved meetings, but in desperation, and the place where they pray is shaken. When they ladle soup to the needy, it is to their own flesh and blood. Service is not tacked-on, it is vocation.

What do we treasure above all else? Scan our checkbooks and our calendar, and you will see. We prize comfort, stimulation, cleverness, amenities, programs, inspiration. We do not give until it hurts. We do not pour out our lives for people who quite frankly make us uncomfortable. As the Archbishop of Canterbury once said, 'Wherever the Apostle Paul went, there was a riot or a revival. Wherever I go, they serve tea.' Membership in a church is rather like membership in a country club, one with very nice teapots. Perhaps it should be more like membership in a gym; we expect to sweat, to strain, to run an extra mile.

Walking purposefully is not reserved for fanciful college students, carefree in the summertime. It is lifelong. It is for the single person, free to live in 'undivided devotion to the Lord' (1 Cor. 7:35). It is for married couples, 'like minded, having the same love, being one in Spirit and purpose' (Phil. 2:2, NIV).[5]

---

5. Chantal and Matt McGee, who run a family retreat center in Colorado, have pointed out that spiritual oneness for a couple requires being on mission together, united in purpose to expand God's rule and reign. Would a man need a "helper suitable" for him if the purpose of marriage was to sit on the couch and watch TV together, Chantal asks? No, men need a helpmate, or "ezer" in Hebrew, because the task to which we are called is monumental. If you are married, you are on mission.

If you are a Christian, you are a missionary.

If, thinking this over, you realize that you really don't have any particular reason to be doing what you've been doing, that in fact it hasn't been very purpose-packed, that perhaps you do have some skills and passions that intersect nicely with a pocket of need on the far side of the world, then what's keeping ya? There may still be a moment waiting for you, a *This is it, this is what I was made for* epiphany, when all that you love and all that you excel at and all that you were meant to be crescendoes, when you look into the eyes of someone who will forever be changed because God made you.

***

There is an equal but opposite error across the fence from a lukewarm life. A life dedicated to saving the world is not quite the same as a life dedicated to Christ, and sometimes the one can sneak up on the other subtly over time. How quickly we become Martha, spending our lives in kitchen service and missing out on the banquet! And this life of service veers off into menial labor, resentment, and great exhaustion before we know it. If the enemy can't keep us from doing something worthwhile, he can double his efforts to burn us out.

Pride is kissing cousins with ministry. If you dedicate your life to changing the world, pretty soon you will begin to believe that you can change the world. You. Not Christ. This is folly, and it is as dangerous for your heart as it is for the souls you seek to save. Service must be overflow or it will be overwork.

Overwork begins with optimism but leads to crushing disappointment. 'If you build it, they will come' only works in Kevin Costner movies.[6]

Overwork is exhausting. It'll dry you out faster than you can say peanut butter crackers.

Overwork is condescending. It says, 'I have all the answers, and I can fix you.'

Overwork begets overwork. Would you pass this ethic to those you serve? 'Serve like me, until it hurts, until you cry out for mercy, until your heart has given out and your first love is lost, and then, if you're good enough, you'll find salvation.' Just say no. God's work didn't begin with you, won't end with you, and doesn't depend on you. Isn't that freeing? If you won't accept rest for your own soul's sake, do it for those who emulate you.

Living on purpose doesn't mean I need to change the world. It means I need to love God. If I offer myself to God, a holy and living sacrifice, I allow Him to set that sacrifice aflame however He wishes.

Oswald Chambers so wisely said,

> We do not need the grace of God to stand crises, human nature and pride are sufficient, we can face the strain magnificently; but it does require the supernatural grace of God to live twenty four hours in every day as a saint, to go through drudgery as a disciple, to live an ordinary, unobserved, ignored existence as a disciple of Jesus. It is inbred in us that we have to do exceptional things for God: but we have not. We have to be exceptional in the ordinary

---

6. Kevin Costner Movie: *Field of Dreams*

things, to be holy in mean streets, among mean people, and this is not learned in five minutes.[7]

Assume, as you set out to walk purposefully through life, that God has called you to obscurity. Assume that you will be a scullery maid in His great castle. Assume that He cares more about the state of your heart than your efficacy, your humility than your reputation, the destiny of the people you reach out to than the impact of your life. Know that at any minute He can do great, unbelievable things in you and through you, that there is no obstacle He cannot surmount and no limit to what He can accomplish by a life that's surrendered to Him. But if you would be Mary and not Martha, keep your eyes fixed on Christ, and don't be distracted by the size of the task. Worship, and it will all stay clear.

Homesick at heart, we all know we were meant for more than bills, duties, sickness, leisure, or boredom. Surely there is more to life than this! If, knowing you are just passing through, you choose to live in light of eternity, you will find the more.

---

7. Oswald Chambers, *My Utmost for His Highest.* (Uhrichsville: Barbour Publishing, 1963) 215.

4: Care Passionately

> [6]*Is not this the fast that I choose:*
> *to loose the bonds of wickedness,*
> *to undo the straps of the yoke,*
> *to let the oppressed go free,*
> *and to break every yoke?*
>
> [7]*Is it not to share your bread with the hungry*
> *and bring the homeless poor into your house;*
> *when you see the naked, to cover him,*
> *and not to hide yourself from your own flesh?*
>
> [8]*Then shall your light break forth like the dawn,*
> *and your healing shall spring up speedily;*
> *your righteousness shall go before you;*
> *the glory of the Lord shall be your rear guard.*

[9]Then you shall call, and the Lord will answer;
you shall cry, and he will say, "Here I am."
If you take away the yoke from your midst,
the pointing of the finger, and
speaking wickedness,

[10]if you pour yourself out for the hungry
and satisfy the desire of the afflicted,
then shall your light rise in the darkness
and your gloom be as the noonday.

[11]And the Lord will guide you continually
and satisfy your desire in scorched places
and make your bones strong;
and you shall be like a watered garden,
like a spring of water,
whose waters do not fail.

[12]And your ancient ruins shall be rebuilt;
you shall raise up the foundations of
many generations;
you shall be called the repairer of the breach,
the restorer of streets to dwell in.

[13]If you turn back your foot from the Sabbath,
from doing your pleasure on my holy day,
and call the Sabbath a delight
and the holy day of the Lord honorable;
if you honor it, not going your own ways,
or seeking your own pleasure, or talking idly;

[14] then you shall take delight in the Lord,
and I will make you ride on the heights
of the earth;

I will feed you with the heritage of Jacob
your father,
for the mouth of the Lord has spoken.'
– Isaiah 58:6-14

He was about twelve years old, skin the color of bright coffee, eyes that shone and a laugh that rang out easily and often. He was gangly, growing upwards faster than he grew out, and he walked with a cocky spring in his step. It was impossible not to love him. His name was Tyler.

Tyler's father was in jail; I do not know why. His stepfathers, all five of them, were also in jail. His oldest sister was sleeping around, eager to drop out of school, scornful of everyone. His oldest brother had joined a gang. Another sister had retreated into a state approaching schizophrenia. One more sister and two little brothers crowded his life. His mother was the devil, I'm pretty sure.

Tyler slept on a couch when he could. There was only one bed in the house, and his mother had claimed it. The kids were usually hungry.

Broken families, crime, immorality, disrespect, violence, mental illness, neglect, abuse, hunger... all these and more have plagued us since Genesis chapter 3. We are far from Eden, far from Home.

When I met Tyler's family, I was twenty-one, and having known them, I could never pretend they didn't exist. Knowledge is responsibility. And to know Christ is to care.

For that reason, it is much easier not to know. In fact, I would advise you to carefully not watch the news, not venture out of your neighborhood, and not ever, ever engage anyone ill-groomed or needy in conversation so as to steer clear of this inconvenience. The Bible is dreadfully pointed on this score: once you see, you are beholden. You see in Scripture that Christ Himself was in raggedy clothes (Matt. 25:35-40), and what you do or do not do with that awareness is a portrait of your heart.

Do you love me? Feed my sheep.

But I digress. My thesis here is not really that you ought to care about the poor; I assume you know that. I want to argue that compassion itself is a key component of an abundant life. Isaiah proclaimed that those who spend themselves on behalf of these downtrodden will see their own gloom turn into midday, their own dark corners fill with light. Not only light, but healing will flow, personal righteousness be gained. You will experience the glory of God, your 'rear guard,' a promise He's got your back. Your prayers answered, His presence near, His guidance available. Refreshment, too: 'you will be a watered garden, a spring whose waters never fail,' your thirst quenched, desires satisfied, delight! You will see restoration come to broken down places, a future established where once were only abandoned dreams. If all of that is not enough, you will soar to great heights – heights of joy, vision, freedom, an eagle carried on updrafts of warm air.

A life spent gazing into a mirror quickly becomes unbearably lonely and sick. We were made to love. A life dedicated to love is ransomed from pettiness, self-loathing, and failure. From darkness to light, from misery to purposeful joy, from drought to abundance, from desert to garden: a life of passionate caring rejects self-centered, atrophied navel-gazing and is gloriously transformed.

When does a real honest-to-goodness saint have time to worry about her outdated wardrobe? Could you sit with a mother at her child's deathbed and fret about your unsatisfactory kitchen cabinets? Love is supremely freeing. It grows and blooms larger than anything else in the room, pushing everything else to the side, crowding out and shrinking down anything less pure, and suddenly the myriad worries and cares of the world have released you, and you are free.

I have struggled off and on throughout my life with depression, a sense of hopelessly weary darkness, a slippery pit of despair. Sometimes it is a by-product of treasonous chemicals dripping into my brain, or succumbing to exhaustion at the end of a long road. Sometimes it sneaks past my defenses in a web of dark lies: you are not enough, there is no way out, God has forgotten you. Sometimes it is pure and simple homesickness, the weariness of longing for a home that seems so far away. However it snares me, there are proven cures. First, I must train my eyes on Christ, doggedly, fiercely, refusing to peer into the alluring darkness. Second, I must love others. Love is a solid place to stand.

To love another person is only possible with Christ. The human heart can conjure pity, fondness, even kindness, but a real love that perseveres in the face of disappointment and does not dissolve into disgust must come from Jesus. Therefore, dare to love your enemy, and you will find your heart filling with Jesus. You will be a vessel made holy by what fills it.

A life full of Christ cannot be a life free from suffering. Would you know Jesus? How can you begin to understand a life poured out like wine, a heart tipped out for the lonely world, and stand detached from love? Love will open your life to heartbreak. You will care when there is no rewarding return. You will see suffering and allow yourself to 'suffer with,' for that is what 'compassion' literally means. You will know rejection, loss, waiting, waiting. It's not all rainbows and unicorns.

To love our neighbors as ourselves is like signing up to be a Red Cross nurse in the middle of a battlefield. We bandage, bring water, pull up the blankets. All around are the casualties of war, deprivation and danger. But like all the brave nurses in all the bloody battles, we press on, because love is stronger than death, hope shines brighter in the shadows, and joy comes in the morning. If this world is all there is, then we are to be pitied. But the day will come when darkness will flee, and all that is broken will be made whole. We fix our eyes on that day, and for now, we love.

The alternative to love is fear. Insulate yourself against the cold, maintain a heart remote and hard. Marilyn Monroe put it this way: 'A wise girl kisses but doesn't love, listens but doesn't believe, and leaves before she is left.' Did Norma

Jean, head tossed in laughter, know an easy life, sunshine without shadow? Those at her funeral would have to admit, 'carefree' had an awfully cold ending.

Perfect love casts out fear. It is risky, reckless, selfless, hard, deep, abiding. Song of Songs proclaims: 'for love is strong as death, jealousy is fierce as the grave. Its flashes are flashes of fire, the very flame of the Lord. Many waters cannot quench love, neither can floods drown it. If a man offered for love all the wealth of his house, he would be utterly despised.'[1] Death, the grave, fire? Not images for the faint of heart.

This abundance Jesus promised is not free from pain, but in spite of pain; it is not easy, but it is good.

Fearless love of others is the natural overflow of a life spent loving Jesus, and the eternal result of a life of love is huge.

***

The author of Ecclesiastes seems to have several pet peeves, one of which comes from the apprehension that all of the lovely, admirable work of his life will fall to dust or ill-use after his death. His vineyards, gardens, parks, gold and silver – meaningless, like chasing the wind. Or as Jesus would later say, 'For what does it profit a man to gain the whole world and forfeit his soul?'(Mark 8:36). The solution to this vexing problem is a change of investment

---

1. Song of Songs 8:6-7

strategy: invest in things that are eternal. Not many things fall into this category, arguably only two or three – the word of God, the human soul.[2]

The naked woman I once saw lying literally in a trash bag on a Manhattan sidewalk: there is something eternal. The lying drunk who begs for your spare change at a busy intersection? That guy's soul is forever. People, irritating, selfish, creepy, manipulative, depraved, or just plain evil, people are the only raw material for everlasting building projects, the kind of architectural wonders that will outlast the Taj Mahal and Solomon's temple by a million, billion years. On Christ, the cornerstone, we are being built into a spiritual temple[3] transcending the decay of time. And in Christ, the widow, the orphan, the immigrant, the poor, acquire dazzling significance.

A life fully lived is a life invested well, storing up everlasting treasure in heaven, not spent on trifles, so that in the end, we won't suffer Solomon's despondence: all that I worked for, gone! An abundant life is joyfully poured out on the lost and the least of these, knowing the eternal value of a soul. In the end, this well-lived life can be

---

2. Personally, I would like to think that there are God-ordained projects He might salvage and improve upon for the world to come – a library of additions to the book of Psalms, say, or a gallery of paintings He quietly inspired, but of course, I've no real proof. I tend to suspect, too, that the best efforts of the best artists on earth will be remembered fondly, like the kindergarten artwork of my children still hanging up on our office wall. 'Aw, remember Buckingham Palace? Wasn't that cute?'

3. 1 Peter 2:5

presented to God unashamed, laid at His feet with a glad heart: here you are, Lord, a gift – a life of love, souls saved along the way.

I spent a few years loving Tyler, his brothers and sisters. I watched with heartache as one by one, they veered down a dark and dangerous path. After school, we'd pick them up, bring them to the church, feed them, tutor them, play. On weekends and summer days I'd swing by and grab whoever was available for ice cream or the park. In the evenings, we'd play basketball with the youth group, laugh a lot, swap lingo. When one of them didn't show up, it hurt a little. When one of them dropped out, it hurt a lot.

After a few years, we moved away, crossing the country with our small collection of odds and ends piled in the back of a truck, watching the city recede in our rear-view mirror and trusting those kids to the King. Over time, I heard reports: a girl pregnant, a boy in prison. No one knew what happened to Tyler; his family dropped off of the radar. We eventually moved back, and I looked for him, not yet to find him. Wherever he is, he took with him a tiny piece of my heart. I mourn, I rail at God. Why did I give my days to those kids, only to hear a stream of endless bad reports? What did it matter, those cookies and juice? So sixth grade went better than it might – who cares if they drop out in tenth?

I see them as I type these words: Maria, her tiny sister Rosa, always ready with a shy laugh, English words slippery on their tongues. Their family, so poor, so transient, has also disappeared. I've no idea what became of them. Jenna, guarded and fierce, the long line of foster homes that did as much damage as the mother with a broom. She lives with her girlfriend and a houseful of children. I don't know if she still loves the Lord, but I know the anger she carried. Jaime, his mind a tangle of confusion and anger – I remember the day he prayed to receive Christ and the day I learned he is serving a life sentence for murder. Their pictures fill scrapbooks and crooked frames in my house. Their lives fill me with questions and tears.

Bob Pierce, the founder of World Vision, cried out, 'Let my heart be broken by the things that break the heart of God.' It is no less than heartbreaking to give your life to broken people and not be able to glue the pieces back together. It turns out, not being God, that I have no power to redeem, transform, or heal. And a life of caring passionately means trusting God to do all of that, trusting Him to follow the ones I love to places I cannot go, trusting Him never to abandon or forsake. It isn't for results that we love, it is for love itself, for Love Himself, who first loved us.(1 John 4:19)

Close your eyes when you give the bum a cup of cold water. You didn't do it for his sneering face, you did it for Jesus. When you pull the sheet over the starving child you couldn't save, remember that the cup of rice you gave didn't fill him, but Christ. When the cell door clangs behind the man all dressed in orange, he isn't walking away alone, but in the presence of a merciful Savior. You can learn more of the love of Christ in the face of one haunted and lost than in a vaulted sanctuary. On the day when at last you see the Son of Man face to face, He has promised to say, 'For I was hungry and you gave me food, I was thirsty and you gave me drink, I was a stranger and you welcomed me, I was naked and you clothed me, I was sick and you visited me, I was in prison and you came to me.'[4] And at last, He will bind up your broken heart, He will welcome you home.

Just after Jesus speaks these words in Matthew 25, the gospel begins its speedy descent to the crucifixion. 'When Jesus had finished all these sayings, he said to his disciples, "You know that after two days the Passover is coming, and the Son of Man will be delivered up to be crucified."'[5] Things are tense. The end is near. The events that follow are poignant in the way that last moments always are in hindsight. As Jesus counts down His final days, a woman arrives at the house where He's staying bringing a beautiful jar of expensive perfume.

'What a waste of money,' the disciples exclaim as she pours it over Jesus. 'He just gave that whole speech about the poor. Think what you could have done with all that money.' But they have missed the point. What you do for the poor, you do for Jesus. And here is a woman who seized the chance to go straight to the top.

'But Jesus, aware of this, said to them, "Why do you trouble the woman? For she has done a beautiful thing to me. For you always have the poor with you,

---

4.   Matthew 25:35-36
5.   Matthew 26:1-2

but you will not always have me. In pouring this ointment on my body, she has done it to prepare me for burial.'"[6] What a moment! She comes to Jesus Himself with her gift, where 'sorrow and love flow mingled down' – a last deathbed visit to one deeply loved, heart in her throat, one last goodbye. What if that ache, that agonizing love, poured out whenever we gave a cup of cold water in His name? Then our love would be a fragrant offering.

**

It is worth mentioning that it is more fun to love people than to hate them, or even to disdain them. Imagine an encounter with someone really wretched, that feeling of disgust and loathing we are immediately tempted to feel. Maybe it is difficult to command your mouth not to sneer, your lip not to curl, your stomach not to sour. Your mind fills with lists of how the wretch has failed, what choices led him down this path. Why should I help him? He will only continue to fall short. He will squander my help and be back here again in a jiffy. No, I will save my pity and my assistance for someone worthy.

Who died and made me the high and holy judge? Pretty sure Jesus' dying was necessary because *I am* that guy. Instead of strutting around like the Prodigal's older brother, I can remember once more the astonishing welcome party thrown on my behalf, the feast, the singing, above all, the Father running to embrace my unworthy self. Ah,

---

6. Matthew 26:10-12

grace. The world is so thirsty for it, needs it so desperately. We received it ourselves, lavishly, and now we can extend it, joyfully, well aware that we are only a pale imitation of a Father whose lip never curled in our direction. We love, albeit so poorly, only because He first loved us.

And oh my gosh, it is fun to dole out grace.

5: Give Generously

I'm convinced that the greatest deterrent to giving is this: the illusion that earth is our home.
Randy Alcorn[1]

Nicolas Cage and Bridget Fonda starred in the 1994 movie, *It Could Happen to You*, the story of a down-on-her-luck waitress awarded a stingy tip: one-half of a lottery ticket. How amazed she was when the ticket won, and the cop who made a promise came back to give her half of the winnings. But the best part of the film is what the pair of them go on to do. Exuberantly, overflowing with amazement

---

1. *The Treasure Principle* (Colorado Springs: Multnomah, 2005), 44.

akin to the Prodigal Son's, they hit the streets and begin giving their money away. The initial gift from policeman to waitress inspires dozens more gifts, from stranger to stranger, all given with infectious laughter and sweetness, none deserved.

It is more blessed to give than to receive. This too, the ability to give, is a gift from God, the very first we see in Genesis. God, as we are introduced to Him for the first time, is uncontainable, lavish, joyful, creative, spontaneous, intimate, bursting with life, wit, and whim. From His fingertips spill star, Saturn, swordfish, platypus, hummingbird, cow, sunflower, live oak, seaweed, Adam. How much was required for a sustainable planet, and how much was just gravy?

God gives, gives freely, gives abundantly, teaches us abundance not by stockpiling the gifts but holding our hand to scatter them all loose in the world, regifting. To give is to spin wild in a circle, child in the father's hands, fearless. Who fears to give when all is manna raining down, inexhaustible?

Seems to me our ability to give joyfully is closely tied to our understanding of who we are. If I see myself as one who's scrimped and saved to rise up in the world, having worked hard for every penny I've earned, I am naturally going to hold on to those pennies pretty tightly. If I see myself as the child of the King, rich beyond measure, living for a little while as a commoner but on my way back to the castle, well, then I may not mind spending some of my pocket change to help someone else along the way. After all, I have an inheritance that will neither spoil nor fade, that no moth can gobble and no burglar can steal.

It is fun to give. Part of the joy of giving comes from the thankful joy of the recipients. Their joy is contagious, passing back to the giver, because, let's be honest, receiving's not so bad, either.

My husband and I have had the dubious privilege of living entirely on a missionary's salary our whole married life, indeed, since before we were married. We began our lives together by spending two months in career missions training, then four months more raising support. From 1998-2005, we were on staff with Campus Crusade for Christ (now called Cru). It is one of the secrets of Cru's enormous success that no one behemoth fund-raising machine is responsible for the salaries of the many thousands of people who serve in the organization. Instead, each staff member begins his or her career on the telephone, making hundreds of phone calls, dozens of personal appointments, logging countless miles to build a team of supporters who give and give and give again to keep the missionary going.

Raising support is a faith-building experience. I've often said that every Christian should do a stint of support-raising at least once in life. Here are a few of the benefits:

One. It becomes abundantly clear to missionaries that God is the supplier of every good thing in life. God puts it on the hearts of lonely widows to send in $10 a month. God puts it on the hearts of wealthy families to donate a car. Perhaps it is tough to remember that your paycheck is a gift of God when it has been issued by a corporation; it is not hard at all when it comes accompanied by letters expressing love and sacrifice. We have been the recipients of money saved up by elementary school children, cancer patients, and one billionaire we've never met. God has answered many desperate prayers when times were tight. Once, we didn't have enough money to buy groceries. A friend appeared on the front porch with a bag of onions and beans. Dinner! Three times our car has died and been immediately replaced by the generosity of our supporters.

Our first home was a ramshackle hovel built 100 years earlier. It crouched in a seedy part of town, slowly disintegrating, before we bought it. The toilet had been leaking so long that when we ripped up the linoleum we discovered the floor rotted right through. How did we not crash to the basement? For a month, we had no toilet, and had to walk to the inner city office where we worked to go to the bathroom. Our front porch was literally falling off of the house. After we moved in, the insurance company announced they'd changed their minds about insuring us, due possibly to the porch, perhaps the crumbling foundation, maybe just the fear of the insurance agent as he drove through our neighborhood.

For a long time, I did not lose heart. We spent our date nights at Home Depot. We dreamed. But when our first son was on the way, my enthusiasm dampened a bit. How could I set a baby on that disgusting floor? We couldn't seem to get rid of the mice. I began to pray, earnestly, for carpet. There was no money left for carpet; the money had gone to fix the toilet and the porch.

A Sunday school class in North Carolina heard about our house and sailed to the rescue. They raised $10,000, gathered a team of eager friends, and flew to Denver. Carpet was not on the agenda. They repaired our back fence, re-tiled our bathroom, painted the whole interior of the house. They brought in beautiful Spanish tile for the kitchen, donated by a contractor. They ate lunches with us on our sagging porch, laughed with us, prayed for us. They met one of our homeless friends, moved to tears when he played the guitar for them: 'Shout to the Lord,' and 'Amazing Grace.' And as they left, they handed us a check. For carpet, they said. They thought we might want some.

The generosity of others has taught us the exceeding value of generosity. Having received, how can we not freely give?

One of my heroes had an incredible perspective on God's ownership of everything. His faith and his generosity were so hand-in-hand that he frequently determined to give away ridiculous amounts before he even saw a farthing of it. Over and over, George Müller saw God work monetary miracles on his behalf. Early in his ministry, Müller felt that God had called him to establish Sunday schools and provide Bibles for the poor. Already he opened his home to dozens of orphans for breakfast every day with barely enough money even to feed his own family. But this new endeavor would cost many times more than the money he had available. So Müller prayed, very specifically, for God to send him twenty pounds to purchase the first batch of Bibles to give away. The same evening, an unexpected knock on the door brought a stranger with an envelope.

'What's this?' Müller asked, and the woman explained. God had put it on her heart and would not give her peace until she brought Him this gift. 'But what is it for?' he pursued. She shrugged, seeming baffled. Whatever Müller thought best? Bibles, perhaps? Without opening the envelope, Müller smiled to his wife. Unless he was mistaken, he would find twenty pounds within. He did.[2]

Not only was George Müller a generous giver, full of faith, but God sent alongside him generous others who supplied the Müller family's needs time and again. If God, the owner of everything, directed George to give his possessions away, George didn't hesitate. God, owner of everything, was amply able to resupply him again.

Every good and perfect gift comes from God.

Two. It's all grace. Living on full-time support makes you very aware of how you spend money. It is, after all, God's money, given in the form of George and Hazel's tithe. What kind of car should we buy? Well, what kind of car would Jesus drive? I have no idea. But I suspect He would be cautious about dropping a year's salary lightly, especially if

---

2.   Janet and Geoff Benge, *George Müller: The Guardian of Bristol's Orphans.* (Seattle: YWAM Publishing, 1999), 98-99.

the choice is between luxury or feeding a town for a year.

And yet. Living on the good graces of other people also puts you in the glare of uncomfortable scrutiny. Is it OK to wear a fancy brand if you bought it at Goodwill? Is it all right to eat dinner out at a nice restaurant when you are weary and need to connect with your spouse? Is it better to save carefully for college and retirement so that we won't have to come round, hat in hand, once again, or better to raise less support now and figure out these little details later?

I bring this up because part of giving generously is letting go of the gift. The gift is grace, unearned. Jesus didn't choose me because of my excellent qualifications, nor do I reflect His heart when I give merit-based stipends. Whether I am giving lunch to a homeless person or part of my offering to a missions agency, I ought to give because the Holy Spirit told me to and let Him use it however He wants to.

Likewise, part of living on grace is learning to set wise boundaries and reasonable budgets and let go of guilt. God gives and God takes away, blessed be His name. His gifts come with no strings attached.

And so, three. Living on support taught us to freely give.

There is a long-circulated story about a missionary overseas who received a box of used teabags in the mail. 'We didn't want to throw them away when we knew you'd be thankful for any tea at all,' said the givers. Really? Is that giving generously?

Are these the acceptable extravagances for one in Christ's service? Used tea bags, maybe a nibbled biscuit?

Giving generously, in the way that will add to your joy in life, means daydreaming before you give. What is the one gift that would make someone smile? How could I go a little further, dig a little deeper? What would delight my friend?

On a trip to Cameroon, in West Africa, my husband was greeted like a king. Everywhere he ventured, the impoverished villagers went all out to make him feel appreciated. Women would spend an entire day scraping out the meat of tiny seeds, mixing them with ground up fish – bones and all – and serving this delicacy with wide grins to the important foreigner at their table. We sophisticated Westerners do not know how to give.

What if you set out today to knock someone's socks off, to bowl someone over? Would you crouch behind the bushes for a chance to see their face, all astonishment? Would you cherish the memory of the day you felt grace flow through you? What if you changed your giving strategy, relied less on formulas and percents and more on the Spirit, the sudden impulse of love? What if you joined the support team of a missionary or two, began to pray for them daily, began to share their joys and sorrows? What if you made a goal to flip your tithe upside down, to give 90 per cent and live on 10? Would God provide for you? Doesn't He now?

God Himself models generosity on page after page in Scripture. Many of Jesus' parables center on giving: the Good Samaritan, the Prodigal Son, the Unmerciful Servant, for example. He highlighted the giving patterns of widows and Pharisees, tax collectors and prostitutes. What was given varied from tangible, monetary gifts to service or love, grace, forgiveness, or mercy. But the heart of the Giver is always abundance. In James, we are told that God gives wisdom 'generously to all, without reproach.'[3] The gift (in this case, wisdom) is not contingent upon some quality of the recipient. Whether or not the person who asks for spare change is worthy, responsible, or respectable is beside the point. Jesus also makes this clear in the Sermon on the Mount: if someone asks for the shirt off your back, give them your coat, too.

We are too sophisticated to take Christ literally. We attend Christian Financial Principles workshops and learn the value of compounding interest. Our money, once set aside, is surely not the money Jesus would have us play around at giving away? We watch the 24-hour news outlets' exposé of phony beggars and determine we won't be taken in by a sob story. Get a job, we sneer at vagabonds.

But there is something magical about grace, the giving and the receiving of it. When we give sacrificially, we echo the gospel again and again, retelling the story of One who gave everything to save a dirty, tattered human soul. Sometimes this might be evident at the moment of gift-giving, but more often, I think, that moment is just a catalyst

---

3.   James 1:5

for the real event of grace that happens in the heart in the hours and days to come. This is especially true if you give directly, not through a third party. Press your twenty dollar bill straight into a dirty and calloused hand, not into the bell-ringer's bucket, and you will see what I mean. Maybe you will see the flash of surprise across a haggard face, the moment when, like Hagar, someone recognizes that God sees. Maybe not.

Have you read Les Misérables, or seen the play? When Monseigneur Bienvenu gives Jean Valjean not just the pile of silverware he has stolen, but the candlesticks, too, Jean Valjean simply gapes at him, too weary to react. Bienvenu did not have the luxury of seeing the transformation take place. It is only later, when Valjean wanders through the town in a fog of confusion, that he begins to understand what the old priest has done.

'Jean Valjean, my brother,' the Bishop had said, 'you no longer belong to evil but to good. It is your soul that I buy from you... I give it to God.' Valjean simply can't comprehend this kind of gift – grace, when he deserved justice, kindness, when he'd extended hate. He staggers through the streets in a fog, wrestling with a lifetime of anger and darkness, resisting this unexpected love. In Victor Hugo's original version, Valjean encounters a happy boy, Little Gervais, who had just unluckily dropped a 40 sous coin, and asks the miserable wretch to help him find it. Even after the old priest's gift, Valjean, unrepentant, steals the child's money. Only after the boy has gone, weeping, does the hardhearted criminal perceive the difference between his own actions and Bienvenu's. His 'heart burst,' Hugo says, 'and he began to weep.'

> As he wept, daylight penetrated more and more clearly into his soul; an extraordinary light; a light at once ravishing and terrible.... He examined his life, and it seemed horrible to him; his soul, and it seemed frightful to him. In the meantime a gentle light rested over this life and this soul. It seemed to him that he beheld Satan by the light of Paradise.[4]

Grace is the mirror which shows our ugliness, and there, behind us in the glass, the reflection of Beauty gazing at us in compassion and love. We see how undeserving we are, and realize again that God's gifts are completely unearned. We see Love.

Grace is a burglar that respects no locks. Grace is nimble with a hairpin, and before we know it, the lock is picked, hard hearts are melting, light is flooding in. Giving generously, graciously, we might just steal the captives from under the jail-keeper's nose.

Giving generously is not an ethic you can work toward, it is a mentality that all is God's; we are not meant to be a dammed pond but a conduit of grace.

We live simply; we give freely. While we are free to enjoy extravagances, the joy comes not from the pampering but from the taste of God's grace, the

---

4.   Hugo, Victor, and Isabel F. Hapgood. *The Works of Victor Hugo*. Vol. 1. (New York and Boston: Thomas Y. Crowell, 1887) 109-110.

reverberating hum, 'I love you, I love you, I love you!' We can as easily find joy in a butterfly on the window sill as a Monet on the wall, as easily find entertainment sharing tacos with a few friends as buying tickets to a Broadway show. When the crazy gifts come, the key to the cabin, the time share in Cancún, we can be blown away, we can say thank you. When we have the opportunity to sell our old baseball card collection and purchase a cow for some starving village, we can be blown away again – *I get to give grace!*

We say thank you.

If this world were home, if this lifetime contained the only days we were given, it would make some sense to hoard our possessions. But the understanding that this is only the prelude to a life richer, fuller, forever, should free us to give generously while we are here. What do we have to lose? If your father is J.P. Morgan, you can spare a nickel . And your Father owns the cattle on a thousand hills! Give away a burger, there's more coming.

6: Hold Loosely

And did thy wealth on earth abide,
Didst fix thy hope on mouldring dust,
The arm of flesh didst make thy trust?
Raise up thy thoughts above the sky
That dunghill mists away may fly.
Thou hast a house on high erect
Fram'd by that mighty Architect,
With glory richly furnished
Stands permanent, though this be fled.
It's purchased and paid for too
By him who hath enough to do.
A price so vast as is unknown,
Yet by his gift is made thine own.
There's wealth enough; I need no more.

Farewell, my pelf; farewell, my store.
The world no longer let me love;
My hope and Treasure lies above.

Anne Bradstreet, 'Upon the Burning of
Our House, July 10th, 1666'

Weary. So weary. They had been through an ordeal – a lifetime of bitter servitude, a season of daily hope-dashing, a narrow escape. They'd rejoiced, but the exhaustion was catching up with them now. For days, they hiked, uncertain of their destination. It was hot; they carried all of their belongings, corralled their children and their livestock, fought the scorching winds. They slept on the hard ground, tossing and turning, gazing bleakly at the vast sky above. They were sticky, uncomfortable, and homesick. What they wanted above all was a home of their own, a place to put down roots, laugh around the dinner table, gather the grandkids, pursue a vocation. But even this grand dream paled in comparison to one nagging irritation: they were hungry. And it was impossible not to complain.

'I wish we had died in Egypt,' said some. 'I'd rather be a slave that eats well than starve in this godforsaken desert,' said others. Moses began to regret being saddled with the whole whiny lot of them, but God had compassion. In the evening, a feast – quail, flocking to be the main course of a campfire picnic. And in the morning, a marvel: during the night it had snowed baklava, honey wafers as far as the eye could see.

'What is it?' they gasped, and gathered it up by the basket, enough for all, but never too much.

'Don't hoard the manna,' boomed Moses. 'More is coming. Use what you can eat during the day, and leave the rest. Trust.' But of course the Israelites didn't listen; who could trust for more? This manna was good. Better to stock up, stash it away, hold tight. And in the morning, mmmm. The manna they'd greedily saved up was maggoty, foul and rancid. What it was wasn't so good any more.

I have been a manna-hoarder. I have gathered my baskets of joy with weary feet and greedy hands. Oh, Lord, so tired, so hungry! And this – what is it? – is so delicious, but so fleeting. How can I know there is more coming?

As John Eldredge says, I have attempted (again and again) to arrange my own little heaven here on earth, but it can't be done. The breathtaking moments won't be snatched, the castles (sandcastles, all) won't stand. The people I love most dearly spring up like wildflowers on a Colorado mountainside and fade away.

One weary day, the weight of a homesick city on my shoulders, we packed a snack and headed an hour out of town, up to Golden Gate State Park in the Colorado foothills. As we drove, I practically pressed my nose to the glass of our car window, 'pierced with many pangs,' longing, *longing* to live in one of the small highway-hugging houses en route to our hiking spot. The yards were generous, spread apart, green, shaded by scrawny aspen and overgrown spruce. Children playing outside could look across the street and up and see deer, see mountain, see nature. No neighbors drunk and fighting. No vulgar graffiti. This was it, my dream. Pack the U-haul, head west.

We quarreled in the car. I was begging, pleading for this dream. I laid out the pros and a couple of cons for the sake of pretending fairness. I listed the health benefits, the parenting plusses, sweetened my words with all the allure of a long-cherished wish. Forfeit our calling? No, no. We could commute. We could office at home – we already did, in fact – we could stack the coffee-house appointments all in a row, we could... But it was not the right time or the right place and I knew it, knew this was a me-plan and not a God-plan, knew it was the bursting of a heart sick with hurts and broken dreams, burnout and battle fatigue.

We'd just had bad news – the kind that feels like betrayal. We'd cried out to God and heard only silence. We'd traveled a long way and still had miles to go. Top it all off with an absolutely appalling tragedy down the street – a movie theater shooting that took too many lives, right there where we'd taken our children to see *Voyage of the Dawn Treader* and *How to Tame Your Dragon* – oh my goodness. I wanted out; I wanted to go home.

We hiked all day, me dragging along behind, realizing numbly that I was missing it all, the white bark against the green backdrop, the laughter of the kids, the sun and shade and wind. It was what I wanted, freedom and beauty and quiet, but like Moses' entourage, I grumbled for more.

I began, as we hiked, to notice the summer wildflowers – Indian paintbrush, black-eyed Susan, fairy trumpet, phlox and flax. I gathered a posy the color of sunrise and sunset, carefully cradled it all along the trail, gently leaned the stems against the cup holder when we made it back to the car, gazed at the bright blossoms as we merged back into six lanes of city traffic, popped them in a vase as soon as we walked in the door. I'd captured my moment, gathered my manna. By morning, all of my flowers were brown and dead.

It doesn't do to grasp for happiness. Happiness is slippery; joy is deep-rooted, firmly planted, reaching deep into a secret source of water and strength to outlast drought and storm. Happiness is fleeting; joy is ever-lasting. Joy, gift of God, is patient – contented, not contingent. God richly gives us all manner of good gifts to enjoy, but not to hoard. Everything under the sun is slip-sliding away.

***

Whatever we gather to answer our hunger will leave us hungry except the Bread of Life. We were made to hunger. Christ, the Bread of Life, nourishing, delicious, satisfying, invites us to feast. Maybe it's because I'm a bakery-loving girl with a sweet tooth, but I love this image of Jesus as Bread. There is hardly anything else in the wide world more wonderful than a fresh loaf – eggy challah, dense pumpernickel, airy croissants, honey wheat rolls, steaming popovers. And the only proper thing to do with such a treasure is to gather around the table with anyone in the vicinity, ooh and aah and pass the butter. Christ offers hearty, tantalizing, down-home goodness. I will satisfy your hunger, He says. Taste and see – I am good.

Maybe the disciples had been pondering this mouth-watering idea for a while when the Last Supper rolled around. What is it to follow Christ? Nothing less than life, rich and full, abundant, satisfying, triumphant. They'd seen this Messiah take the bread, give thanks, break it, feed 5,000. Enough for everyone. Peter might have thought, Let's get Jesus to make us some snacks to sell at a mountaintop rest stop. Heaven on a plate. But then the picture changed a bit.

This is my body, Jesus said at that final meal, startling them (again). He lifted it up, gave thanks, broke it. Take, eat. Do this in remembrance of me. Now the Bread of Life was the bread of suffering, of sacrifice. It was Passover; the lambs had been slaughtered, the blood painted on the door; everywhere the smell of roasting meat rose smoky in the air. Jesus was not just the bread, He was the Lamb.

Like Peter, like the Israelites, I would like to hoard the manna, pop up a tent on the mountain, savor the bread. I would like to avoid the sacrifice, loss, and heartache. I have got to learn to hold loosely.

Not everyone agrees. 'Hold fast to dreams / For if dreams die / Life is a broken-winged bird / That cannot fly,' wrote Langston Hughes. There is something to be said for hanging on tight, especially to dreams. It is difficult to maintain a dream through drought and storm, and the hope attached to the dream can slip away. But really, the dream isn't what we need to hang on to, it is the giver of dreams.

***

God, giver of dreams, once gave a dream to a man named Abraham. Dream of a child, He said. Dream of a boy to make you laugh. Dream of grandchildren, one for every constellation in the sky. The years passed, the dream seemed unattainable. Abraham tried to help God along, arrange for a miracle. That was a bust. Hagar, Ishmael, the whole embarrassing debacle was the result of Abraham's and Sarah's volunteer event-planning on God's behalf. But God had a bigger event in mind. Finally, finally, the dream came to pass – a child, laughter. Still God wasn't through. Just when Abraham relaxed into a happy retirement, God spoke again. Lay the dream on the altar, commanded the dream giver. Give it up. Sacrifice your son.

What did Abraham love more, the gift or the giver? Could he trust the heart of a God so shocking? Or would he grab on a little tighter, hold fiercely to the dream, to the child, to the love? Abraham holds the boy loosely, and clings to the Father. His faith is astonishing.

Have faith, we say flippantly, scrolling the word in pretty font on shower curtain and tissue box. We've gotta have faith, faith, faith! sings George Michael.

Writer Virginia Stem Owens says,

'No one, I'm convinced, should be allowed to claim faith who knows where his next meal is coming from or where he will sleep tonight. Faith is a word we should fear to have on our lips, lest it be defined for us in ways we cannot imagine. Kierkegaard would go farther. You should not talk about faith, he would say, unless you are prepared to stand, like Abraham, with the knife raised over your child's body.'[1]

Um, not so sure about that kind of faith. Can I get a refund on that shower curtain?

Owens goes on to say that Abraham might have obeyed, woodenly, with resignation, yet without faith. That is to say, he might have hardened his heart against God even while he stood prepared to kill the dream. 'The problem with resignation, as opposed to faith, is that it kills joy... Resignation can only receive its children back again with pain. Only faith produces joy.' Had Abraham not believed in his gut that God was good and trustworthy would his act of obedience have been bitter and cold? Could it have wounded his love of God permanently?

I know about resignation. Climbing sadly back into the car, driving with a sigh back up the driveway in the city, looking at the distant purple ridge and wishing I were there. OK, God, I have said with a loud exhale, here I am. Obedient Kate. Killing the dream. Go ahead, God, you can have it.

---

1. Virginia Stem Owens, "Søren Kierkegaard: Desperate Measures," in *The Classics We've Read, The Difference They've Made*, ed. Philip Yancey (New York: MultiMedia Communications/McCracken Press, 1993), 71. Owens, writing about Søren Kierkegaard's classic, thoughtfully unpacks the Danish philosopher's work, applying it to her own circumstances.

This is not thankfulness. It isn't faith, or joyful surrender. It's my deep mistrust of the heart of the giver concealed under the facade of dutiful doing. Clearly, it's not holding loosely, it's a pity party, a poisoned pity party at that, fed by devious whispers as old as Eden. God is holding out on you, Satan still hisses.

Yet God is the giver of all good gifts, who gives more than we could ever ask for, hope for, or even imagine. He gives the desire and then fulfills it in grand style, heaped up, pressed down, running over. He brings me to the banqueting table, and His banner over me is love (Song 2:4). When it seems I have to give up the dream closest to my heart, I have to remember the character of the sovereign God of the universe. He has not abandoned me nor forsaken me, forgotten my prayers nor ignored my needs. I am simply asked to treasure Him first.

Interestingly, the story of Abraham's great test follows closely on the heels of the cautionary tale of Sodom and Gomorrah found in Genesis 19. Lot and his family, cozied up to sin in a lifetime of compromise, were forced to flee for their lives, give up their possessions, friends, and dreams as their infamously wicked homeland burned to the ground. The surrender was not so freely given in their case; Lot's wife, unable to let go, turned back with longing to gaze at what she'd lost. We do not know her name; we remember her as she died, a picture of misplaced desire, a pillar of salt – thirst, unquenchable. Her legacy to her daughters was also desire, corrupted. Living with their old, defeated father in seclusion, the daughters longed for Life. Rather than bring this request to God, they seduced their father, daughter-initiated incest, bearing sons whose descendants (Moabites and Ammonites) were the sworn enemies of Abraham's descendants for generations.

Lot's wife could not let go, because she did not hold loosely, and did not trust in a loving Father to provide. Abraham, on the other hand, did not regard the son he loved as his own possession in the first place. Tears in his eyes, he raised flint above his precious child to literally sacrifice this dream to God. '[B]ecause you have done this thing, and have not withheld your son, your only son, indeed I will greatly bless you, and I will greatly multiply your seed as the stars of the heavens, and as the sand which is on the seashore; and your seed shall possess the gate of their enemies. In your seed all the nations of the earth shall be blessed, because you have obeyed My voice,' declared the Lord.[2] Through the faith of a man surrendered to God, through his radical trust and posture of openhandedness, the whole world has been blessed. Anything Abraham thought he would have to give up was given back to him, multiplied, enriched, magnified. And God was greatly pleased.

The gut-wrenching obedience of Abraham is a beautiful picture of the gospel: a son given for sacrifice. Whenever we give our cherished treasures to God, we hear the echo of all that was given for us; we remember that He, not sparing His own Son,

---

2. Genesis 22:16-18, (NASB)

graciously gives us all good things. Usually our own holding loosely is not nearly so painful or dramatic. Prying our fingers from the little idols hurts, but not much, not for long.

Generally the challenge to hold loosely hits me in the nitty-gritty, minute-by-minute choosing to let go of my expectations – not the grand dreams, but the 'hey, I was supposed to have a minute of peace and quiet here!' How often my day is spoiled because someone else's need edges in on my plans. What I most frequently grasp too tightly is my freedom, my perfect schedule. Me first. Putting it in perspective – life is short, all is God's, I'm just here to serve – can help. If I stay alert for divine appointments, regard nothing as interruption, I can roll with a little grace. Nate Saint said, 'If God would grant us the vision, the word sacrifice would disappear from our lips and thoughts; we would hate the things that seem now so dear to us; our lives would suddenly be too short, we would despise time-robbing distractions and charge the enemy with all our energies in the name of Christ.'[3] Whoa. This is a guy who gave it all. What's a little interruption in comparison?

But I'm just gonna be honest here, it's really hard to put that into practice. Even without realizing I'm doing it, I'm making plans. What rises up inside me, day after day, is selfishness, which is why I need to be filled with Spirit, rooted in Spirit-love and

---

3. Elisabeth Elliot, *Through Gates of Splendor*, (Massachusetts: Hendrickson Publishers, 2010).

letting Him produce Spirit-fruit: patience, peace, gentleness, and my favorite, joy. Fill me up with joy and I won't need to go grabbing for it.

***

This summer I've been spending extra time meditating on John's metaphors for Jesus. Earthy, simple, profound, beautiful, and endlessly thought-provoking, these word-pictures have added richness to my prayers and my understanding of God. They also train me to let go.

- Hold loosely to my possessions, because Jesus is the Bread of Life. He will satisfy my deep needs.

- Hold loosely to my wishes, because Jesus is the Living Water. Drink deeply, and I will never thirst.

- Hold loosely to my expectations, because Jesus is the Vine. If I am still, He will produce fruit.

- Hold loosely to my home, because Jesus is the Good Shepherd. He will lead me, feed me, protect me, guide me, take care of me, welcome me into green pastures.

- Hold loosely to my family, because Jesus is the Lamb of God. He has already given more than He will ever ask of me.

It has been a long road. God called us to plant a church in a downtrodden suburb of Denver, and we – assumed. Assumed God had big plans for us, and by that, big plans for our church. And what are the big plans of God if not for miracles and wonders? We have been flummoxed by the glacial slowness of God, His quiet refusal to act in the ways and according to the timetable we set for Him. We have suffered setbacks, and more setbacks, discouragement, attack, frustrations, confusion, and the deafening silence that greets our desperate prayers. Yet God did not release us – we were stuck. That summer of the shootings was our low point. But in the middle of a hard, hard season, good news. We were given the chance to take a sabbatical, our first big break after thirteen years of ministry.

So we found ourselves in Massachusetts, a time to reflect, a time to study. It was balm for our scrapes, rest for our weary souls. We met with God, heard His voice again, walked by the quiet waters. It was a gift – not the one we were looking for, but nevertheless a huge, amazing gift. Still, it was fleeting.

We toured historic sites in Boston, Plimoth, Stockbridge. We stood in an Ipswich Cemetery and marveled over graves from the 1630s. Our guide was Dr. Garth Rosell, a professor of church history from nearby Gordon-Conwell Theological Seminary. Under the canopy of trees, he read off headstones and told us of the lives hidden beneath the etched names. Here a pastor from the earliest settlement, there a wife, 'most amiable companion' to her mate. Pointing to one of the many original houses lining the Ipswich streets (now with Volvos parked out front) he told us that once upon a time, Anne Bradstreet lived there.

Freshman English class came rushing back; Anne Bradstreet was our earliest American poet, one of the only women to be published in that day and age. Known for her devoted love to her husband she led the charge for women writers. Dr. Rosell pulled out a worn book and read her words to us there in the solemn cemetery, reminding us of the incident that led to the poem. When, in 1666, the Bradstreet home burned to the ground, Anne and her husband Simon lost everything, including her precious library of books. She wrote,

> And when I could no longer look,
> I blest His grace that gave and took,
> That laid my goods now in the dust.
> Yea, so it was, and so 'twas just.
> It was his own; it was not mine.
> Far be it that I should repine.

Standing there where the roots of great old trees coil around ancient bones beneath the earth, Anne's words had great resonance. None of her possessions were really her's, and the house crumbled to ashes was not really her home. She understood. Even as she stood under the dark sky and smelled the smoke of her treasures rise to blot out the stars, she knew it was never hers to keep. She lifted her empty hands and surrendered it all to the Lord.

Anne held loosely her dream of home. Could I?

So quickly our time away wound down. The little bubble of time, suspended above and separate from our life, was thinning, thinning, ready to pop. And then it was over. We were going home.

Home – the thing I want above all, the ache for it sinking deep into everything I do. Madeleine L'Engle said, 'We are all strangers in a strange land, longing for home, but not quite knowing what or where home is. We glimpse it sometimes in our dreams, or as we turn a corner, and suddenly there is a strange, sweet familiarity that vanishes almost as soon as it comes.' Of course, the home we were heading to after sabbatical didn't feel like home, wasn't really Home at all. It was certainly not my dream of a mountain cabin, but having rested, I felt more able to relax into it than I had for a while. There in Massachusetts, I pictured the light (Jesus, Light) filtering through the tree in the front yard, fresh-baked bread (Jesus, Bread) steaming on the table, Mrs. Burns lingering in the driveway to chat. Maybe we would find joy in that little house. Maybe we could practice hospitality in that tiny kitchen, find beauty through the front door.

Jesus, Door, can we enter through you into our house every time we enter; can we dwell in you? Jesus, Peace, will you always be waiting when we arrive?

I have had to hold loosely to my assumptions, and lay on the altar my grand dreams. Doing so, I can breathe a little easier. I feel the stirrings of hope. And better than all the homes I could ever construct on a Colorado mountaintop, a Home waits for me, shining on a hill. I'll try to wait.

In the meantime, I pray with A.W. Tozer.

The man who has God for his treasure has all things in One. Many ordinary treasures may be denied him, or if he is allowed to have them, the enjoyment of them will be so tempered that they will never be necessary to his happiness. Or if he must see them go, one after one, he will scarcely feel a sense of loss, for having the Source of all things he has in One all satisfaction, all pleasure, all delight. Whatever he may lose he has actually lost nothing, for he now has it all in One, and he has it purely, legitimately and forever.

'O God, I have tasted Thy goodness, and it has both satisfied me and made me thirsty for more. I am painfully conscious of my need for further grace. I am ashamed of my lack of desire. O God, the Triune God, I want to want Thee; I long to be filled with longing; I thirst to be made more thirsty still. Show me Thy glory, I pray Thee, so that I may know Thee indeed. Begin in mercy a new work of love within me. Say to my soul, "Rise up my love, my fair one, and come away." Then give me grace to rise and follow Thee up from this misty lowland where I have wandered so long.'[4]

---

4.   A.W. Tozer, *Pursuit of God.* (Pennsylvania: Christian Publications, 1993), 19-20.

7: Love Deeply

I love my husband. I love my children, my parents, my friends, my dog. I love Swiss Chocolate Almond ice cream, cabins, and canoes. I love church, and I love people (some of them, anyway) in the church. I love books, authors, poets and singers, aspen and foxes, wildflowers and mountains, the beach. I love the lost and the least of these, the poor, the sinner, the hero, the saint. I love Jesus.

How in the world can one word contain all of that varied, broken, holy, burning, yearning, sweet, enduring love? I say that we must love deeply in order to experience life rich and full, in order to mitigate the homesickness that threatens to make us lose heart. But what do I mean?

It's all love, isn't it – all of the wholehearted worship, generous giving, compassion and care and service? All that we do in obedience or holiness or wonder is love boiled down and refined, in all of its various expressions and forms, just as every candy or pie or pudding is really just sugar. Worship is *agape*, unconditional and deep, the highest love of the highest object enabled by Spirit and sustained by grace. Compassion is *agape* overflowing and hopefully mixed with a little *phileo*, friendship; it is directed vertically but spills over horizontally, fountain-like.

We seem to have an instinct for friendship that doesn't require too much instruction, and a deep sense of duty, as Christ-followers, to 'love' the lost and hurting (although we need rather more prodding and damage-control in this category). Love for God is something we will never in all our days perfect; if we had endless ink, parchment, quill, we could never write an adequate love song to the Savior. But two sorts of love I haven't much yet addressed deserve a bit of further exploration: one, because we would often prefer to avoid it, the other, because we frequently neglect it.

The love we like to skip over is so fundamental to Christianity that our bungling of it has put the entire church in peril, crippling our witness to a watching world. It is, of course, love for Christ's body, His bride, the church.

New Testament writers are crystal clear on this point: to love God is to love His children. There are no alternatives. If you are a follower of Christ, you cannot hole up in isolation and love Him solely through prayer and meditation. To commit to Him is also to make a selfless commitment to love the others He gave His life to save. Participation in Christian community is not a perk, it's a pre-req. Unfortunately, while it's not too difficult to suspend judgment in regard to nonbelievers, it can be insufferably hard to live out the seventy times seven bit for a brother. He should know better by now! He should be transformed! What is his excuse?

We are a graceless lot. Eager to receive forgiveness, stingy to give it, we lose patience. Clearly, we have good reason: the church is beset by politics, quarreling, pettiness, ugliness. Humans. Surely it does not please God to hear the old crows bicker about music or to listen to the singles gossip. We would rather escape, commune with God in nature, or just in private. We stand aloof, distancing ourselves from the mess. It is the old gnosticism, equating spirituality with sublime thoughts and higher knowledge, insisting that Jesus was more God than man, that we can ditch the earthly and seek a higher plane. Course, we don't call it that. We accuse the church of falling short, failing us, wounding us. We leave to lick those wounds in peace. We don't notice that we surround ourselves with people just like us, with shiny mirrors who reflect back to us what we most want to see, what we most secretly worship, ourselves.

To love the church is to love the whole church. Beggars, addicts, womanizers, cougars, yuppies, snotty children, the old, the irrelevant, the stupid, the ugly, the materialistic, moralistic, opportunistic, the selfish, the arrogant, the cheaters, the liars, the holier-than-thous. There is no escaping. To say otherwise is to say you are better, holier, closer to God. Are you closer to the One who suffered and died for them? Then you will die, too. Most likely your 'suffering' will be putting up with them, your dying will be to yourself. But it's the only way.

John, the disciple Jesus loved, is our most vocal instructor on this subject. Let him rip:

- 'if we walk in the light, as he is in the light, we have fellowship with one another, and the blood of Jesus his Son cleanses us from all sin' (1 John 1:7)

- 'whoever says he is in the light and hates his brother is still in darkness' (2:9)

- 'whoever loves his brother abides in the light' (2:10)

- 'whoever does not practice righteousness is not of God, nor is the one who does not love his brother' (3:10)

- 'everyone who hates his brother is a murderer' (3:15)

- 'by this we know love, that he laid down his life for us, and we ought to lay down our lives for the brothers' (3:16)

- 'let us not love in word or talk but in deed and in truth' (3:18)

- 'anyone who does not love does not know God, because God is love' (4:8)

- 'if anyone says, "I love God," and hates his brother, he is a liar; for he who does not love his brother whom he has seen cannot love God whom he has not seen' (4:20)

If you haven't read I John recently, you'll think this is an exhaustive list; believe me, I just reported a small sample. Dear old John goes on and on, walking around and around his subject, studying it from a thousand angles. The test of your walk with God, says John, is whether and how and to what extent you love your brother.

In the meek and lowly places of the world, where to be a Christian is to invite persecution and expect execution, the body of Christ is a shelter. To love your brother and be loved in return is to share your possessions freely, to protect your sister fiercely, and to daily die to self. After all, what is death to selfishness in light of the threat of actual, painful death? Christians in Nazi-occupied territory risked everything to hide families in the attic, to smuggle food off their own tables to share with the needy, to whisper of hope. We choose from a smorgasbord of churches according to shiny performances and nifty programs, staying only as long as our 'needs are met.' We don't even know what our real needs are. (Are you wise enough to choose spinach and broccoli at an all-you-can-eat buffet replete with every indulgent, delicious option the chef could devise? Can you choose to love the unlovely when presented with an alternative?)

Introduce heaven into the equation and see what happens. First, this world is not my home, this is not perfection on a plate. It is not forever. It is not all there is. I am looking forward to something much, much better. Perhaps I can endure a while longer. Second, whether I have wrapped my brain around it or not, I am in basically the same situation as the persecuted brothers in enemy-occupied territory – I am an alien and stranger here in the thick of a great battle. If I am engaged in this battle, I will need the refuge of the church. Love will sustain me. If I do not perceive this need, maybe I am not really engaging the fight. And third, when at last I do come home, how I've loved Christ's bride is going to be a big deal to Him. The One who sees and judges the thoughts and intentions of my heart is certainly going to zero in on this: did I love well? Did I live to be served or to serve?

Ask not what your church can do for you... Why might the annoying lady need you? Why might the weary KidZone worker want to see you stay? What could you learn from the stinky guy, the needy family, the clingy friend? So what if your pastor is more heartfelt than eloquent, the worship team more devoted than talented? We eyeball the trade of authentic for flashy, broken for plastic. In search of perfection, we accept phony as a reasonable substitute, until at last this fails us, too, and we simply give up, withdraw, and retreat to worship ourselves.

I grant, it's easier to speak lofty words than to practically apply this teaching. There are legitimate reasons to seek a new congregation; would Jesus require anyone to indefinitely reside in Laodicea, for instance, or allow us to shake the dust off and look elsewhere? Still, I wonder what percentage of church-goers these days change churches because of genuine zeal for holiness versus just... boredom. Perhaps we have unwittingly trained a generation of believers to be consumers, a byproduct of church marketing strategies, clever new programs, and glossy, perfect services.

To love one another deeply, from the heart, to bear one another's burdens, to sharpen one another as iron sharpens iron, to rejoice with those who rejoice and weep with those who weep, to so bind our fate to another's that we stand together or fall together, this is a recipe for endurance, character, and hope. This is the kind of love that causes the world to wonder, all astonishment, what could possibly account for it. What would motivate Handsome and Wealthy to spend his free time with Socially Awkward and Broke-Down? How is it that in time of crisis, we bear up with grace and peace, supported by a loyal tribe of faithful, oddball friends?

The very oddness of truly Christlike community is perhaps its strongest witness. Nowhere else in our society would passersby witness the voluntary, joyful gathering of such a disparate, ragtag group, drawn not by the trendy but the true. It is the kind of love that might just compel someone to ask the reason for the hope we have. No wonder we aren't asked more often.

And this kind of love ought to transcend denominational lines as well. Do you count among your friends Calvinists, Pentecostals, high church, low church, Catholic and Protestant? It doesn't matter if your brother whoops it up in a suit and tie or reverently kneels in flip-flops to take the bread and the cup; after all, someday soon we will all be bowing before the throne in humble recognition that we got it wrong as often as we got it right. If you find that you are too often stuck in a small bubble, you might consider getting out more. Go find a soup kitchen to serve in, or an old-folks home to visit. Mingle with some Christians in another context. It'll do you good.

As it happens, loving others is a remarkable antidote to pride. A momentary shock at the deep wisdom or faith of a homeless man, or the opportunity to be quietly served by someone you regarded as vacuous and vain, these little reminders that we don't hold the corner on godliness or insight leave us a bit meeker, a little less pretentious. It's also impossible to be an 'ear-tickler' in love. You don't say what people want to hear in order to look good or win friends, you say what really needs to be said regardless of the consequences of your own bluntness. How often we can trace an awful moral failure back to a self-aggrandizing attitude – maybe we can guard against these things by ramping up authentic love.

The way of love is humble, patient, self-sacrificing, and forgiving. It is not needy of others' good opinions, not fearful of condemnation, and not self-protective. Love is utterly unselfish. It doesn't matter what others think of me as long as I am thinking of others.

The temptation to abandon love in order to make a good impression, attract non-believers and grow a church is ever-present in full time Christian ministry. Which is a better church-growth strategy: to drive out of your way to pick up an obese disabled man every Sunday morning or to spend those precious minutes picking up free Starbucks to offer newcomers? To allow the monstrously talented, hip guitarist to lead worship or to confront him for being sexually promiscuous and let the weird off-key lady warble out the hymns? Love is the more excellent way, but don't say I didn't warn you. It's liable to take a whack at your high society reputation.

***

There's another love to plumb the depths of if you would live life rich and full. It's altogether more fun than loving your enemies, a homework assignment you might actually enjoy. Who sits with you at the breakfast table? Love the heck out of them.

Paul admonishes singletons in 1 Corinthians 7 to embrace this freedom and live in undivided devotion to the Lord. I wonder if perhaps single people are able to achieve an intimacy with God generally unknown to married folks: God is the Beloved, True Companion, Friend. A single person not continually hunting for a partner is apt to lean on Christ's breast out of necessity, undistracted, single-minded. He is the go-to confidante, the conversation partner at dinner, the one to please.

Unattached to anyone else, a single gal can experience 'God is my portion' the way a thirsty runner gulps water in relief. Whether you haven't been married yet, used to be married but aren't any more, or never intend to marry at all, your single status is an opportunity to experience God's love at a radical level and a chance to serve Him with complete abandon. Don't miss it. Treasure it.

Still, a bachelor is someone's son, someone's friend, someone's brother. There are as many opportunities to dive into love as there are people in your life, and this love will add to your joy and enrich your days. Just because you aren't half of a salt and pepper set is no reason not to love deeply and sacrificially. A love that demands something of you and asks nothing in return will inevitably make you more like Jesus.

And yet, for the majority, we work out our salvation in the context of marriage and family. And this unique set of relationships is in itself a high calling, and an incredible opportunity to tap into deep, deep joy. What's not a good idea is to squander. This is not the place in your life to go half-heartedly.

If you've taken the leap to unite yourself to someone else, this love has got to be second in importance only to God Himself. It's not a 50-50 proposition, whereby you give 50 per cent and hope the spouse chips in their half; you have to give it all, always, not holding back, and trust God to refill you. You give patience, kindness, thoughtfulness. You hold your tongue when it would be so easy to jab. You don't criticize when you justly could. You choose not to be crabby. You put the lid on the toothpaste and don't throw your stinky socks on the floor. You put up with indignities, have faith, keep no record of wrongs. You believe the best.

These things we know. But still, we slide. We slowly let work schedules and to-do lists define our days. We do not guard our time. Soon our spouse has gotten used to being on the back burner. We settle in. We have been hurt, we hold back, we protect ourselves. We find distractions, avoid the hard work. We choose resignation.

Living in an attention-deficit afflicted society does not help. It is hard to turn off the TV, turn away from the Internet. We give our hearts to lesser things – not all at once, of course, but slowly, over time. Soon it is rare to have a meaningful conversation. We forget to pray together. We forget to dream.

The secret of great love, so widely forgotten, is known by the lilies of the field. Up they pop every spring, a profusion of color and dazzle, joyous and free. Not fussy or anxious, not modest but exuberant, unashamed, they lift their heads to bask in the sun, they dance in the breeze, they drink in the dew. For just a moment, they live, fully, abundantly. And then they are gone. Such are we, here for a moment only. Look across the breakfast table. That person sipping coffee, nibbling a muffin, will vanish from your sight like a mist, like the spring flower show outside your kitchen window.

When you recognize the constraints of life 'under the sun,' in which heartache and sickness and troubles abound both for the godly and the wicked, the rich and the poor; when you realize that you are simply a traveler here, an alien and a stranger in a land not your home; when you begin to understand that this very day might be your last, look again at that person passing the butter. Sweep the plates from the table and seize your beloved, smother them with kisses, cancel work and spend the day on a blanket in the park. Life is short. The one you love is temporary.

> I perceived that there is nothing better for them than to be joyful and to do good as long as they live; also that everyone should eat and drink and take pleasure in all his toil – this is God's gift to man.... Enjoy life with the wife whom you love, all the days of your vain life that he has given you under the sun, because that is your portion in life and in your toil at which you toil under the sun.[1]

The Teacher, from Ecclesiastes, after years of study, has come to several related conclusions. Life after Eden is a long troubled road. We fight the weeds in the garden, the rocks in the soil. We toil to make salad grow. When at last we have a plateful to gather and sit down hungry to dig in, someone wicked is apt to come along and take what we worked for, eat it his lazy self. We work to live a righteous life. We choose integrity, passing up ill-gotten gain. Our neighbor, the bum, cheats and lies his way to the top. A for sale sign goes up; he is moving to nicer digs. Meanwhile, the sewer backs up, our house is flooded. Such is life.

---

1. Ecclesiastes 3:12-13, 9:9

But we're not all poor and troubled. A few of us are in fact quite rich. An honorable man lives to a hundred years old, surrounded by adoring children, lucky in health and wealth. But is he happy? No, never content. He dies, leaves his wealth to the grandkids. He would have been better, says the Teacher, never to have been born at all.

We long all our lives for meaningful relationship, seek it high and low. When at last we commit to another, we find ourselves locked in a power struggle. The glow of new love fades. Serve her? Submit to him? But the Teacher is clear: of all the gifts God gives under the sun, chief among them is love.

Figure out a way to find joy, to find meaning in your work. It is better in the end to be wise, better to be just, better to be industrious than foolish, oppressive, or lazy. The value of life isn't in prosperity or success, but in its intrinsic virtue, a life God sees and will reward when we finally go home. So go ahead, build the vineyards, get the Ph.D. There is nothing wrong with enjoying life. But mostly, love. Because 'If one person falls, the other can reach out and help. But someone who falls alone is in real trouble. Likewise, two people lying close together can keep each other warm. But how can one be warm alone? A person standing alone can be attacked and defeated, but two can stand back-to-back and conquer. Three are even better, for a triple-braided cord is not easily broken.'[2]

Your spouse is a gift, a friend and companion for the journey, a warm presence and comfort,

---

2. Ecclesiastes 4:10-12 (NLT)

a source of strength. Your love is made in the image of Trinity God, a dance of giving and receiving, serving and encouraging, adoring and basking in adoration. Braided into Christ, you become a cord of three strands, stronger together than you could be alone.

Choose a life less busy, a calendar clear. Guard your time. Guard your affections. Where do you spend your money? Where do you spend your days? Where do you give your heart? Guard that heart, it is the wellspring of life. Protect oneness with your spouse. Guard against drifting. A frenetic schedule, misplaced priorities, a life chock full of tempting and expensive distractions, a few secrets shared with the wrong person, and soon you have drifted impossibly far. Paddle. Don't give in.

The best practice I know of to strengthen your marriage and sink your roots deep into joy is to pray together. Daily. Grab a hand and acknowledge, every day, that your life is not your own. You are on mission together – check in with your field commander and get your marching orders. Thank God for this most amazing gift – the gift of companionship, of being deeply known by another human being, of being cherished; thank Him that you both lived to see another day. Looking on your spouse in wonder (what beauty God creates! what strength He bestows!) should only increase your wonder in God Himself. Give God your love once again, and ask Him for His own love to fill and empower and overflow from you. Do this, and your marriage will be long-lasting, sparkling, and secure.

Neglect it, and statistically, your odds of making it plummet.

Now, it seems to be fairly common among the married to acquire along the way a small flock of ducklings that happily squawk and waddle around after Ma and Pa. For roughly eighteen years, each of the little ducks has been entrusted to your watch and care. What we tend to forget is that the little whipper-snappers don't belong to us – their true Father is in heaven. We are the chosen guardians of God's child. Handle with care! No other person will so deeply impact your kids, except possibly their spouses. Most likely, you will not arrange their marriages – their spouses they will happily choose for themselves. You, they didn't get to pick. They're stuck with you. And in two short decades, you will define their view of God, their view of themselves, and their potential.

Survey your friends – how many have a warped view of God because their earthly fathers were unforgivingly severe? How many avoid their mothers because they smothered them, not getting the love they needed from the dear old dads? How many children do you know who act out because they get no attention at home? How many will not be held accountable for their flagrant sins because their parents didn't bother to discipline? We know the horror stories, see them daily played out on the news, tragedies traced back to godless parenting. None of those 'bad parents' set out to bungle things. They failed to regard their children with appropriate awe and their job description with wonder. They slid by.

What would it look like to have a family lit up by love? What if Ma and Pa adored each other, adored their children? What if your schedule was dictated by the highest good and not expedience, by a sense that today might be your last day on earth instead of by the lazy assumption that you've all the time in the world? What if your life was not busy, but full, not helter-skelter, but unhurried? What would you do every morning? Every evening? On a day off?

I know a dad who bakes bread with his daughters, laughing, flour-dusted. Together they slide the buns from the oven and sell them to raise money for hungry children overseas. I know a mom, eyes always merry, who homeschools her kids on a mountaintop, takes time to sled down the long snowy driveway, follows Dad around the world on missions trips to Romania. My husband is in the next room right now, playing a board game with my children while I write. They wade across rivers together, whittle, read stories, skip rocks, build snowmen or sandcastles, have tickle wars. Every day he reminds me, *grace*. Make love the bullseye. Pray.

We stayed in a cabin, an hour from civilization, snug in a valley that should be on postcards. Across the street was a sledding hill, really a long and twisting driveway. The hike up it is asthma-inducing; to stand at the top and look back you feel it's quite impossible you made it up at all. The kids loved nothing better than to drag up sleds and fling themselves back down. There comes a moment when you sit on the devil-may-care device and feel the world beneath you begin to slip – and you're off. Once you're going, there's no stopping (short of a crash); none of your shrieking makes a difference. Our kids are like that – teetering on the edge of a thrills-and-spills ride from innocent childhood into their own great adventures. I see the world beneath them start to slide, the sled is moving, none of my shrieking can stop it.

They say busyness is the great enemy of marriages: hurry, worry, distraction from what really matters. The simple things, intentionality and care, are too hard to cultivate when you're running 100 miles an hour. It's not just marriage, it's anything slow and painstaking – the spiritual life, the writing life, your very heart. Feed it rush and scramble, watch it wither. We are under the illusion that we control our calendar and own our possessions. Ha! We're like the Harry Potter Villain – Lord Voldemort, divvying up our soul into precious pieces and thinking, spread out, there is more of me to go around. Be careful where you stash your life.

The clock cannot tell me how to live my minutes. I choose. And today I choose to savor, even as the world is whipping by. I won't be rushed, won't give in to worry, hurry-scurry. Today is a gift, and though tomorrow everything may change, today I have children I don't have to nag, battles I can pick, a husband I can lavish with love, a view I can stop to see. All of my fears won't add a minute to my life, so I show them the door.

What is the chief end of man?
> To glorify God by enjoying Him forever.

What is the chief end of marriage?
> To glorify God by enjoying Him forever, together.

What is the chief end of parenting?
> To glorify God by teaching your children to enjoy Him forever.

'Train up a child in the way he should go; even when he is old he will not depart from it.'[3] What do we train our children to do? Obey? Serve? If your goal is to have well-educated, well-behaved children, you will train them very differently (and your family will be quite different) than the one whose goal is to have children who enjoy the Lord.

Cultivate wonder in your children, make your home a chapel of praise. Give thanks, always, with a glad heart. Look for God's fingerprints. Treasure God's Word. Treasure each other. Live for eternity.

In Colorado, where it is sunny 300 days a year, solar energy is a sensible way to go. Just by existing in the hot, dry climate you can power the hair dryer, the Christmas lights, the blender. But like a sunflower, a building that's solar-powered will thrive only if the solar panels face the sun, drink it in. Orient your life towards the Son, drink Him in. He will fill your family with light, with love. He will power you.

It's not a small thing, you see, to craft a vision for your family around the enjoyment of God.

---

3. Proverbs 22:6

It must reorient all that you do. Make decisions according to that rubric – what will help us to enjoy God together? What kind of vacation should we take, for what are we saving our money, what are we watching, which extracurriculars do we sign up for, what fights are worth the cost? Only what will help us enjoy God together. Wow.

I grew up in an evangelical culture that frequently tweaked that goal just a bit. We tried our very best to *please* God by avoiding sin. We talked a lot about holiness – I don't smoke, drink, or chew, or go with girls who do. We evaluated our decisions accordingly – how many bad words can be in a movie before it's too bad to watch? And watch out for sex, it might lead to dancing! It seems such a small shift, to focus on pleasing God or to focus on enjoying God, but can you see how different are the results? It never occurred to me that there was a difference until, in college, I encountered John Piper's work. Oh my goodness.

If you strive to enjoy God, you'll probably want to please Him, too – you'll hate what He hates and love what He loves. But you'll also live a life of amazement, delight, freedom. If you focus on avoiding sin, you can miss that. It is similar to the difference between not killing your enemy or loving your enemy. Hey, I'm right there with you, Pharisees. Killing the enemy, not good. But how much better is love? And how much more difficult?

Choose in your family to enjoy God together. Lavish love while you can. We aren't given much time.

8: Stand Firm

We are so utterly ordinary, so commonplace, while we profess to know a Power the Twentieth Century does not reckon with. But we are 'harmless,' and therefore unharmed. We are spiritual pacifists, non-militants, conscientious objectors in this battle-to-the-death with principalities and powers in high places. Meekness must be had for contact with men, but brass, outspoken boldness is required to take part in the comradeship of the Cross. We are "sideliners" – coaching and criticizing the real wrestlers while content to sit by and leave the enemies of God unchallenged. The world cannot hate us, we are too much like its own. Oh that God would make us dangerous!

Jim Elliot[1]

The Lord, who sends thee hence, will be thine aid;
In vain at thee the lion, Danger, roars;
His arm and love shall keep thee undismayed
On tempest-tossed seas, and savage shores.

John Newton to Richard Johnson[2]

I live in a city in the middle of America. It is bold and brash and self-important, a city of great beauty, great wealth, and high culture. There are myriad parks full of beautiful people jogging, dozens of theaters and museums full of applause. The city sits in the shadow of incredible natural wonder in a state that can astonish even the most hard-hearted. Some of the world's greatest athletes play here for millions of dollars. Some of the world's greatest minds gather at her hospitals and universities. And citizens from all over the world flock here in hope of a new life.

It is a city of incredible darkness. Only 5-10 percent of the people here fear the Lord. How many who die in this place awake to find themselves dragged into hell?

If we had eyes to see, we would see people staggering, blind, bound, lost, deluded. We would see

---

1.   Elisabeth Elliot, *Shadow of the Almighty* (New York: Harper Collins Publishers, 1989), 79.

2.   Josiah Bull, *John Newton of Olney and St. Mary Woolnoth* (London, UK: The Religious Tract Society, 1868), 287.

Satan prowling like a roaring lion, seeking to devour us, choking the life from all who enter (1 Pet. 5:8). I believe we would apprehend immediately that this great city is central to a diabolical master plan. It is like quicksand, sucking masses of people to their death.

We would see, amidst the darkness, pinpricks of light – a remnant of God's children. In some places, a small cluster of lights, mostly in the nicer parts of town, but generally just a sprinkle. And if we zoomed in further, we would see a tremendous battle surrounding every flickering flame. Yes, evil clutches and bites, but there are also warriors doing battle on our behalf. No Cupid with his diaper and a flimsy bow and arrow – great beings, mighty, breathtaking. The host of the Lord of Hosts, soldiers whose occasional appearance in the Bible is always accompanied by a hasty 'Do not fear!' Like Elisha's servant, we would take heart.[3]

But the forces of darkness hate the light. Satan is not lazy; he is vicious and relentless in his attack. He curses and screams obscenities at God's people, he entices and seduces, he accuses and he mocks. At every turn he waits in ambush, desperate to retain his hold on this city, desperate to steal, kill, destroy and snuff out each little candle-flame.

We are God's chosen people, holy and dearly loved. We live in this city of darkness with its poisonous fumes and we hang on for dear life so that we will not be driven out. But oh! We have

---

3. 2 Kings 6:8-18

been chosen and appointed by God Himself to rescue the dying, to drive out the devil. Chosen by God and appointed to His service – commissioned to this battle. We struggle not with flesh and blood, but with the very sword of God against the god of this age. (Eph. 6:12, 2 Cor. 4:4)

Every victory is bloody, every loss is heartbreaking. But we dare not forget that more is at stake than our small concerns. Every setback distracts us from the deeper reality of what is going on. We are a tiny 'band of brothers,' a tiny group of rebel soldiers in an evil empire. We have to circle up, back to back, armor on, and fight.

Maybe, like Sodom and Gomorrah, this city will crumble and burn in its own vileness. But perhaps, like Nineveh, it will fall to its knees, and a great light will flood the darkness, and the devils will howl.

Though we are weary, we can't forget the stakes. We are tempted every day to listen to lies from that schemer, Satan:

- Give up, go home, I've already won.
- God has forgotten you – you are all alone!
- You can still salvage your personal happiness if you leave all of this behind.
- You don't have what it takes.

But GOD says:

- I have given you weapons divinely powerful for the destruction of strongholds. (Based on 2 Cor. 10:4)

- I will never leave you nor forsake you. (Heb. 13:5)

- You are the salt of the earth! You are the light of the world! (Matt. 5:13-14)

- Though you are small and weak, you are precious and honored in my sight, and I love you. (Based on Isa. 43:4)

- I have chosen the weak things of this world to shame the 'wise.' (Based on 1 Cor. 1:27)

- In this world you shall have tribulations, but I have overcome the world! (John 16:33)

- I know your deeds. See, I have placed before you an open door that no one can shut. I know that you have little strength, yet you have kept my word and have not denied my name. ... I am coming soon. Hold on to what you have, so that no one will take your crown. The one who overcomes I will make a pillar in the temple of my God. Never again will they leave it. I will write on them the name of my God and the name of the city of my God ... he who has an ear, let him hear (Based on Rev. 3:8,11-13).

If we had ears to hear, eyes to see, we would see the finish line – and we are almost there. We would hear the cheers, the roar of encouragement from a great cloud of witnesses (Heb. 12:1), a multitude who were faithful, who have gone before us. And we would fix our eyes on Jesus, who long ago survived a bloody battle and won for us forever a bright and unwavering victory – Jesus, who stands waiting for us with open arms, a wide smile, and a 'well done.'

Oh, God, give us eyes to see!!

***

If, looking for a life that is rich and full, you have determined to take up your cross and follow Christ (worshiping wholeheartedly, caring passionately, loving deeply, walking purposefully), you cannot expect to live this life unchallenged, any more than you could walk into Nazi territory with a big sign reading, 'I'm here to liberate the Jews!' and expect Hitler to hand you the keys to the concentration camp. Indeed, you had better expect the opposite, or you will be in for a shock. As J.R.R. Tolkein wrote, 'It does not do to leave a live dragon out of your calculations, if you live near him.'[4]

Unfortunately, this battle is generally more sly than swashbuckling, and you may be down for the count before you take a swing.

It's interesting to study the great wars of history and take note of the numbers of men and women who've died without ever firing a shot or even being fired upon. In the Revolutionary War, it was soggy shoes. In the Civil War, starvation. During World War I, trench fever. In World War II, frostbite. Young boys who lied about their age to join the glorious battle died in heaps from flu, malnutrition, malfunctioning weapons, exhaustion, or friendly fire. And in spiritual battle? How often will you face down a demon, brandish a Bible, and boldly declare, 'In the name of Jesus I command you to leave!'? More likely, you will wake up one day and despair, 'Why am I here? Why do I bother?'

4. J.R.R. Tolkein, *The Hobbit*. (New York: Houghton Mifflin Company, 1997), 195.

The weapons used against us are mental and emotional. You will be lied to. You will be accused of failure. Your sins will be shouted in your ear without reprieve. You will be opposed by the most unlikely people, surprised by betrayal, worn out by criticism, made to feel ridiculous. You will be weary. And if Satan does his work well, you will give up and go home, disengage from battle, succumb to compassion fatigue, find that you have lost your first love, your joy has dried up, and you are too exhausted to hope. All without ever realizing that you were in a battle in the first place.

The Accuser goes after the heart, the wellspring of life. As John Eldredge has said, '[I]t is in our heart that we first hear the voice of God and it is in the heart that we come to know him and learn to live in his love. So you can see that to lose heart is to lose everything.'[5] And what has the enemy done from the beginning? Targeted our weak and unprotected hearts.

> 'Eve, your good friend God over there has been holding out on you. He does not give good gifts. He does not have your best interests in mind. He wants to rule you, not to love you. He is stingy, unkind, oppressive. You are smart enough to figure this out: ditch God and make some decisions for yourself! Be empowered.'

> 'Cain, God loves your brother and not you. How is that fair? You are being cheated here, and

---

5. Brent Curtis and John Eldredge, *The Sacred Romance*. (Nashville: Thomas Nelson, 1997), 3-4.

judged unfairly. You are getting a raw deal. That smarmy little jerk – you would be so much better off without him. No one will ever know.'

'Elijah, way to go on that whole Prophets of Baal Showdown! That was awesome. Of course, now Jezebel is going to totally kill you. All your dreams came true, everything you ever prayed for in ministry, and it's kind of a let-down, isn't it? You're going to have to run for your life, all alone. Here you do all these miracles, and nothing ever changes. They just don't get it, the idiots. You could stand on your head and juggle fireballs all day and they'd never change. If only there was anybody who could understand. But you're all alone. Alone. Alone.'

The list goes on. Jonah, David, Sarah, Esau... all the victims of lying schemes that went straight for the heart, to the tender spots, easily poked. Satan preys on jealousy, resentment, desire, real human need. He goes for the wounds we lick, the scabs we scratch over and over again. It is too easy.

The only remedy is to Boy Scout up and be prepared. Guard yourself, be alert, awake! It's impossible to be defeated by a surprise attack if you are not surprised. Resist the devil, and he will flee with an angry howl. Stand firm, therefore.

The Helmet

I have noticed Satan's propensity to speak in the first person. Perhaps a theologian of a certain bent would disagree with me, point out that my own heart is deceitful and wicked, capable of a thousand treacherous thoughts. He would not be wrong. I am desperately sinful. But I think from time to time the thoughts that assail me, surprise me, aren't actually my own thoughts at all. *I don't have to put up with this crap*, says one, angry, so angry! And sometimes I chime in, *Yeah. That's right. I don't have to take this from you!* Often that particular mean-spirited voice purports to stand up for me in a heated argument, an inner cheerleader rooting for division and strife.

A more winsome voice seduces at other times, *Beauty. What I need is more beauty, a little peace and quiet. Serenity.* It is the voice of my idols, the things I long for more than I long for God, the things I would replace Him with. It is sweet, gentle, cajoling. Hard to identify, harder still to resist. It would be easier if it came in the second person: *You know, Kate, what you really need is to quit your job and move to Belize.* Ah ah ah! I am on to you, Liar! But masquerading as my own dream, he slips past my defenses. Maybe I need some better armor.

Pop on a helmet, says Paul in Ephesians 6, the helmet of salvation.

What has your salvation procured for you? Meditate on this: you have been born again to a living hope, an imperishable inheritance that is kept in heaven for you, unfading. No – first person. *I* have a living hope! *I* have an imperishable inheritance! I must teach myself to speak truth, to speak it loudly and often, over the clamor of my own deceitful heart and the lies of demons. The Lord is my Shepherd, I shall not want!

Who is not assailed by fear and discouragement? And if you were the devil, what would you do to a saint at that moment? I'll tell you what I'd do. I'd tell the saint he suffers because of his weakness, he is destined to fail. I'd remind him of all the times he's blown it before, and inform him that God has finally given up on him. I'd search for the God-ordained trials and try to exploit them for my advantage, twist them like a knife through the heart. But the testing of our faith is not designed to disprove our salvation or disqualify us, it is intended to produce perseverance. Hold me, Jesus, and I will come out like gold through a fire.

A living hope, an imperishable inheritance, the unflappable mercy of God – none of these things can the devil touch. He can make me doubt, but he can't separate me from the love of God. This 'putting on the helmet of salvation' is a declaration both to myself and to the enemy that I will not be shaken. I will stand my ground. It is like glaring across the battle line and giving a war cry: You will not take me alive!

The Breastplate
Meditation on salvation protects our imagination, but what of our softly thumping hearts? Once a lie has lodged in our grey matter, it doesn't have far to travel to infect with poison our deep heart's core. And so Paul says to strap on the breastplate of righteousness. I think if I'd had to guess what protection our hearts need, I would have come up with something akin to the 'breastplate of love.' What better to protect our emotions than love? But Paul knows of a frequently used and powerful lie

and its proven affect on our heart, and it is against this lie that he arms us. Maybe Satan will say that you are unloved, but the truly terrifying corollary to that humdinger is this: you are unworthy of love. Because of your ridiculous, continual mistakes, you have lost God's love. Here is a lie I can believe, because I have met me.

No, you aren't perfect. Satan will accuse you (fairly accurately – it's not a stretch) of all kinds of failure, but Jesus knew those things about you before He saved you, before you even committed those sins.

It's a pretty common human trait to be surprised by our own sin. Like the Emperor, we strut in our silly birthday suit and brag about our awesome outfit. When we chance to pass a mirror, it is a shock. But God is never surprised. He saved you *anyway*. He dunked you in His holiness, and when God looks at you, He sees clean white perfection, the Lamb of God, who takes away the sin of the world. It is Christ's righteousness, not our own, that protects us here.

Defeatism will take you out of the battle, but the memory of how God sees you – beloved and pure – not only wards off depression, but gives you someone to fight for, resolve to carry out what He began. Meditation on sanctification jumpstarts our motivation.

The Belt

You had better be prepared for lies from the Great Deceiver, so buckle up. Learn to listen for the lie and respond with truth. Hmm, God has forgotten me? Not true! *He will never leave me nor forsake me.* I am all alone? Not true! *God is a father to the fatherless and protector of widows.* Lies are awfully effective when undetected, but quite impotent unmasked.

Recently my husband's friend advised him to consider what lies he might have internalized over the years and list them out. Lies? Surely not. And yet, pen in hand, he began a list that grew startling, a list of false accusations stored up over decades, unnoticed, like weeds entangled in a garden. Uprooting the stubborn beasts is a delicate business.

And so my husband knelt on a snowy Colorado riverbank and wept over his list of lies. One by one he struck them out, confessed the partial truths twisted amongst them, renounced the falsehoods and their insidious power. One by one he dealt with them, asking Jesus to heal the infected wounds they left behind. The list he ripped to pieces and flung into the river. Tumbling icy water carried it away. A healing began. He called it a Eustace and Aslan moment.

What he refers to is one of the loveliest moments in the Chronicles of Narnia. Eustace, a disagreeable boy if ever there was one, has turned into a dragon. And though we are short on pity for Eustace, Aslan is not about to leave him the same way he found him. Eustace needs healing. In fact, Eustace needs an identity overhaul, an 'extreme makeover.' Bringing the dragon to a pool, the great lion says to undress and bathe. Undress? wonders Eustace. Of course, as a dragon, he isn't wearing any clothes. But then he thinks about reptiles shedding their skins, and begins scratching off the scales that cover him.

Much to his disappointment, he finds layer after
layer of hard, dry skin needing to be removed, and
the more he scratches off, the more there seems to
be to do. Finally, Aslan offers to finish the job.

I was afraid of his claws, I can tell you, but I was
pretty nearly desperate now. So I just lay flat down
on my back to let him do it.

The very first tear he made was so deep that
I thought it had gone right into my heart. And
when he began pulling the skin off, it hurt worse
than anything I've ever felt. The only thing that
made me able to bear it was just the pleasure of
feeling the stuff peel off. You know – if you've ever
picked the scab of a sore place. It hurts like billy-
oh but it is such fun to see it coming away.

Well, he peeled the beastly stuff right off – just
as I thought I'd done it myself the other three
times, only they hadn't hurt – and there it was
lying on the grass: only ever so much thicker, and
darker, and more knobbly-looking than the others
had been. And there I was smooth and soft as
a peeled switch and smaller than I had been. Then
he caught hold of me – I didn't like that much
for I was very tender underneath now that I'd no
skin on – and threw me into the water. It smarted
like anything but only for a moment. After that it
became perfectly delicious and as soon as I started
swimming and splashing I found that all the pain
had gone from my arm. And then I saw why. I'd
turned into a boy again.[6]

---

6. C.S. Lewis, *The Voyage of the Dawn Treader*. (New York:
HarperCollins, 1994), 109.

Lies from a dragon have dragon-power to change us. They get in through a mental doorway and proceed to infect us at a heart-level. Eventually, if they aren't caught and yanked quickly enough, they alter how we operate and even who we are. We need God to claw down deep into the soil of our soul and pull them out, one by one. Hurts like billy-oh, but it's worth it.

The Shield

Satan's fiery arrows will fall thick and fast upon you, seeking an unprotected spot. In ancient times, arrows were frequently smeared with pitch and set ablaze, so Roman soldiers, anticipating this, commonly soaked their huge wood and leather shields in water before heading into battle. A shield isn't much good when it's on fire, but a shield so saturated literally snuffs out flaming arrows. Paul, observing as he did the regiments of soldiers who guarded him under house arrest, described our 'shield of faith' in similar terms, able to extinguish all of the devil's flaming darts.

You have faith? Great. You have a shield. But is it a shriveled, burnt-out faith, or living and active? Dive into the Living Water and swim awhile. Spend time with the wellspring of life. If you don't, your faith will become dry and brittle, easily ignited by one of Satan's missives. Soak your shield.

Does Satan question God's character? That arrow will fizzle out against a faith soaked in Exodus 34:6-7, 'The Lord, the Lord, a God merciful and gracious, slow to anger, and abounding in steadfast love and faithfulness, keeping steadfast love for thousands, forgiving iniquity and transgression and sin, but who will by no means clear the guilty...'

Does he question our ability? Our effectiveness in ministry? The genuineness of our walk with God? These doubting darts are no match for 2 Corinthians 12:9-10, 'My grace is sufficient for you, for my power is made perfect in weakness. Therefore I will boast all the more gladly of my weaknesses, so that the power of Christ may rest upon me.'

If you can begin to trace a pattern in the lies used most often against you (and I imagine they are different for every person), you can build up an arsenal of verses ready to counter-strike. Choose a few that speak powerfully to your heart and wrap yourself in their cover. Read them before you set out every morning. Tape them where you can't avoid seeing them. Hide them in your heart. And this brings us to 'the sword of the Spirit, which is the word of God.' If you would advance and not retreat, you will need an offensive weapon, and this is it.

The Sword

There is a scene in the wacky film classic, *The Princess Bride*, which perfectly illustrates the sword of the Spirit. For many years, a Spanish orphan sought revenge for the death of his father, practicing sword-fighting and learning to duel with the best, until at last he tracks down the villainous six-fingered man who'd killed his dad. Nearly dizzy with delight at the prospect of avenging this murder, Inigo Montoya rehearses what he will say when he meets his foe. Gleefully he chases his opponent through a castle until, rounding a corner, he is greeted by a flung dagger and sinks to the floor in agony. Braver now, the six-fingered man taunts him, mocks him, slices him twice before raising his sword to finish him off. Suddenly, Inigo's steel flashes, and he wards off death, rising slowly to his feet and declaring out loud what he'd intended all along to say: 'Hallo. My name is Inigo Montoya. You killed my father. Prepare to die.' The fight is not over; the duel continues, and with each swing of his sword, Inigo repeats the words again, louder and louder, until the enemy shrieks, 'Stop saying that!' Though weakened by wounds and staggering in pain, Inigo is not defeated; his sword seems suddenly to wield a strength of its own, fueled by a triumphant shout of victory.

It's easy to spot a Christian who's been on the losing end of spiritual battle. Slumped in the corner, eyes dull with pain, she lies still while the enemy circles, taunting and striking unopposed. When she opens her mouth, the words that come out aren't her own, they are lies internalized and regurgitated. But hand her a sword, let her swing it, watch the enemy retreat. Speak out the truth, shout it loud; the devil will tuck his tail and run, bleating over his shoulder, 'Stop saying that!'

The sword of the Spirit is the *rhema* – the spoken word of God. By all means, read it, understand it, meditate on it, and memorize it, but then you have to *use* it. 'For the word of God is living and active, sharper than any two-edged sword, piercing to the division of soul... and marrow, and discerning the thoughts and intentions of the heart.'[7]

The Rear Guard

Interestingly, Ephesians 6 does not record any armor for the back. It seems fleeing is not a recommended option for the believer. But in Isaiah 58:7-8, we are given some consolation. The glory of the Lord is your rear guard. It is God Himself, commander of angel armies, who will watch your back. And of course, no matter how we prepare for battle, ultimately the battle belongs to the Lord.

> [W]ho is a rock, except our God? – the God who equipped me with strength... He trains my hands for war, so that my arms can bend a bow of bronze. You have given me the shield of your salvation, and your right hand supported me, and your gentleness made me great.... For you equipped me with strength for the battle; you made those who rise against me sink under me. [8]

God aims His bowstrings and routs the evildoer; God is our rock and our fortress and our deliverer; God is our shield, our stronghold, who saves us from the wicked with His sword. God holds the keys of death and hell. 'His eyes are like a flame of fire... He is clothed in a robe dipped in blood... From his mouth comes a sharp sword... On his robe and on his thigh he has a name written, King of

---

7.   Hebrews 4:12
8.   Psalm 18:31-32, 34-35, 39

kings and Lord of lords'[9]. If God is for us, who can stand against us? Not a one.

The nineteenth century missionary John G. Paton repeatedly experienced God's protection among the cannibals of the New Hebrides (now called Vanuatu) in the South Pacific. Many times he was threatened by angry armed men – no idle threat, since this same people group had slaughtered and barbecued the first pair of missionaries on the island in 1839.

In his autobiography, Paton recounts one such occasion:

'My heart rose up to the Lord Jesus; I saw Him watching all the scene. My peace came back to me like a wave from God. I realized that I was immortal till my Master's work with me was done. The assurance came to me, as if a voice out of Heaven had spoken, that not a musket would be fired to wound us, not a club prevail to strike us, not a spear leave the hand in which it was held vibrating to be thrown, not an arrow leave the bow, or a killing stone the fingers, without the permission of Jesus Christ, whose is all power in Heaven and on Earth. He rules all Nature, animate and inanimate, and restrains even the Savage of the South Seas.'[10]

---

9. Revelation 19:12-16

10. Quoted by John Piper in his message, "You Will Be Eaten by Cannibals! Lessons from the Life of John G. Paton" given at the 2000 Bethlehem Conference for Pastors and recorded on desiringgod.org. From p. 207 of *John G. Paton: Missionary to the New Hebrides, An Autobiography Edited by His Brother* (Edinburgh: The Banner of Truth Trust, 1965, orig. 1889, 1891).

Paton understood the invisible power of God in the face of the very visible, tangible power of His enemies. How much more should we trust in God's protection without the rattling of sabers in our face?

The spiritual giants of the past all knew the stakes and dove into the battle undeterred. They realized, as we must, that nothing great can possibly be accomplished by those who are idly standing by. Whether our engagement of spiritual battle is on a foreign mission field, at the local supermarket, or on our knees, we still require the same attitude of alertness, confidence, and determination. And we are not alone.

Paton's story reminds me of a tiny parenthesis tucked into 2 Samuel 5:23-25. David's army is suited up for battle with the feisty Philistines. 'Shall I go up against them?' David asks.

> And when David inquired of the Lord, he said, 'You shall not go up; go around to their rear, and come against them opposite the balsam trees. And when you hear the sound of marching in the tops of the balsam trees, then rouse yourself, for then the Lord has gone out before you to strike down the army of the Philistines.'

And so David's men crept in among the evergreens, and waited. There in the stillness of a shadowy forest, inhaling the heady fragrance of resin, they waited. And then, a breath, a whisper of breeze. The tops of the trees began to sway. The wind gathered, whooshed. The sound of marching, the host of heaven, the Spirit of the Living God had come.

The battle belongs to the Lord.

9: Choose Light

Thankfulness Hymn

for the small things: light on water, shaded
   forest, laughter ringing
clear my mind to see your beauty
make me thankful, Lord
for the moments gone forever, conversations, love
   so fleeting,
give me power to remember,
make me thankful, Lord

all the gifts declare your kindness,
joyful Father, loving Friend,
make me long for you, my portion
sweeter, higher, without end

for the shocking incarnation, setting glory to the side,
Jesus, King come as a baby
make me thankful, Lord
for the shocking death you suffered, love propelling
* Love to die,*
Jesus, King killed as a pauper
make me thankful, Lord

all the gifts declare your goodness,
humble Savior, loving Friend,
make me long for you, Redeemer,
sweeter, higher, without end

for the breath of God upon me, blowing through
* me, to renew me*
in my weakness, grace unstinting,
make me thankful, Lord
for the suffering, give me vision of your purpose,
* of your wisdom*
tease out meaning, comfort me
make me thankful, Lord

all the gifts declare your mercy,
tender Spirit, loving Friend
make me taste your kind compassion,
sweeter, higher, without end

for the final destination, journey ending, sailing home
rest and healing, joy and beauty,
make us hopeful, Lord
for the moment we will see you, hear you calling,
'welcome home!'
feel your arms in love surround us,
make us hopeful, Lord

all the gifts declare your brightness,
glimpses in the dreams you send,
make us thankful for a future
sweeter, higher, without end.

Instinctively, humans have always known that caves are creepy. Hundreds of years ago, everyone knew that caves are where the dragons live. When Slovenians discovered foot-long salamanders deep in the dark, they knew – *knew* –that the creepy-crawlies were baby dragons. Centuries-old pictographs of scorpions and spiders warn off spelunkers at the mouths of caves in the Sierra Nevadas. *All hope abandon, ye who enter here.* Any schoolchild can tell you that bats live in caves; bats, they will add, are vampires.

National Geographic reports,

> 'Cut off from the fruits of photosynthesis, most caves are places of hunger. Yet, most depend indirectly on the sun. In some caves, like Hurricane Crawl, rootlets from trees far above dangle through cracks in ceilings, providing bug food. Leaves and twigs wash in on spring floods from nearby connected creeks. Rodents penetrate surprisingly far, bringing seeds and nesting material. Bats also come and go, leaving behind guano, and their dead. Occasional 'accidentals'—big animals like raccoons or snakes—wander in but don't wander out, providing banquets that may stoke the food chain for centuries (in one Sequoia cave, debris and bones are piled a hundred feet deep in a pit trap).'[1]

---

1. Krajick, Kevin. 'Discoveries in the Dark.' *National Geographic.* National Geographic Society, September 2007. Web. August 1, 2015.

Hunger, darkness, stagnation, death. Troglobites, creatures living in caves far below ground, have lost the ability to see, not only blind, but eye-less, alert for the skittering sound of a potential meal, but unable to see what they consume.

Creepy, right?

A cave-dwelling critter might very well be free to leave its home and strike out for the sunlit world above, but it never would. Troglobites prefer darkness.

We are not so different, you and I.

Plato wrote about this curious characteristic as well. Suppose, said the old philosopher, that a group of prisoners were chained to the wall of a cave. Shackled at the legs and neck, they could not turn their heads, but were able only to see shadows on the wall before them. Suppose that behind the prisoners, a fire was lit for their warmth, and between the prisoners and the firelight, a parade of characters walked by, carrying sundry objects, all of which cast shadows on the wall. The prisoners, watching this shadow theater, would have no knowledge of the real people and objects dancing by, and would mistake the shadows for reality. A man carrying a dog might appear to be a two-legged being with a dog's head, for example; a woman with a pot balanced on her noggin might look to be a giant. If then, said Plato, one of the prisoners were released, and turned around, wouldn't he be astonished to see what cast the elongated, flickering shadows? And if he were lead up, up, into daylight, wouldn't the bright sunshine hurt his eyes? He would wince and cower, shield his face, perhaps retreat back into the world of shadow.

Gladly, we are not shackled, though we begin our lives in that very cave, adjusted to the darkness, watching illusions and mistaking them for truth. We are indeed free to simply turn around and walk out of darkness and into the light. Some of us do walk out, join the radiant life that is really life above ground. Many of us never will. But then there are those who begin, a little tentatively, maybe, to exit the cave, walk blinking up the corridor, but shrink back at the noonday glare. Too bright! We are troglobites. We prefer the dark.

Part of seeing eternally, seeing well, is stepping out into the light. It is a choice.

And there it is, the practical part. In light of eternity, choose. Choose to leave your cave, blink into the sunlight.

What will you meditate on, hours on the highway, life whipping by? Will you set before your heart what is temporary or dream about what is eternal? This choice is the difference between hope and despair, between light and dark. It is a choice. We fix our eyes.

In Colossians, Paul reminds us of this. The Message puts it this way:

> So if you're serious about living this new resurrection life with Christ, act like it. Pursue the things over which Christ presides. Don't shuffle along, eyes to the ground, absorbed with the things right in front of you. Look up, and be alert

to what is going on around Christ—that's where the action is. See things from his perspective. Your old life is dead. Your new life, which is your real life—even though invisible to spectators—is with Christ in God. He is your life. When Christ (your real life, remember) shows up again on this earth, you'll show up, too—the real you, the glorious you. Meanwhile, be content with obscurity, like Christ.[2]

Other translations are more commanding. Set your heart, set your mind, seek the things above. Choose, choose, choose. Choose you this day whom you will serve. I have set before you life and death; choose life!

My parents have on the wall of their family room an old-fashioned cuckoo clock. A pendulum patiently tocks the seconds, a springing bird chimes the hours. This clock must be set each day or it will not keep time. Weighted pine cones hang below; these must be pulled to reset the gears inside. If the clock is not reset, it will grind to a slow halt, stuck. If it's come to a stop, someone has to check it against a correct timepiece and start the whole thing over – adjust the hour and the minute against reality and begin again. How similar is the human heart! It must be maintained, reset, daily. If it is not carefully tended, it will soon lose track of time, stop feeling the weight of time. Eventually, realizing it is hopelessly stuck, its owner will have to adjust it, consult a true standard, force it to comply. Only a heart properly set is reliable or helpful for anyone.

---

2. Colossians 3:1-4 (MSG)

But set according to eternity, it beats out a steady rhythm of love.

Setting heart or mind on things above means cherishing things above, meditating on things above, fixing your attention on things above. It happens through prayer and pouring over God's word, asking questions like: How can I better align my actions with this truth? Which of these options is eternally significant? How would God have me spend these hours? What is the gift in this circumstance for which I can give thanks? The resulting state of mind is not only more purposeful, but decidedly more joyful.

What you stare at will define you, what you think about, you will become. That's why the self-help gurus will tell you to write out your goals, tape them to the bathroom mirror. Ask an Olympian. If you want to shave a second off, you must recite that resolve every day. But it isn't just Chicken Soup for the Soul. Jesus preached it, too, with a Jesus-y, infinite wisdom twist.

> Do not lay up for yourselves treasures on earth, where moth and rust destroy and where thieves break in and steal, but lay up for yourselves treasures in heaven, where neither moth nor rust destroys and where thieves do not break in and steal. For where your treasure is, there your heart will be also. The eye is the lamp of the body. So, if your eye is healthy, your whole body will be full of light, but if your eye is bad, your whole body will be full of darkness. If then the light in you is darkness, how great is the darkness![3]

---

3. Matthew 6:19-23

What do you treasure? The thing you gaze upon. To set anything less than God Himself before your eyes is idolatry, and will fill your vision, your body, your life, with darkness. To fixate on your worries will just make you into a big sour stew. But to dwell on things eternal? Joy. A 'healthy eye' lets the light in, fills a life with clear, bright light. If then you find that your life seems dingy, dark, scary, and sad, perhaps it has to do with what you are gazing at. Maybe a change of scenery is in order.

In Philippians 4, the imprisoned apostle Paul draws a strong correlation between peace and perspective.

> Rejoice in the Lord always; again I will say, rejoice. Let your reasonableness be known to everyone. The Lord is at hand; do not be anxious about anything, but in everything by prayer and supplication with thanksgiving let your requests be made known to God. And the peace of God, which surpasses all understanding, will guard your hearts and your minds in Christ Jesus. Finally, brothers, whatever is true, whatever is honorable, whatever is just, whatever is pure, whatever is lovely, whatever is commendable, if there is any excellence, if there is anything worthy of praise, think about these things. What you have learned and received and heard and seen in me—practice these things, and the God of peace will be with you.[4]

I like the progression of thought. Rejoice, prisoner, because the Lord is near. Rejoice, you who suffer.

4.   Philippians 4:4-9

Can you see Him? Well, He's there. So don't worry. Why worry when the Lord is near? Surrender. Bring that list of concerns to the One who is able to take care of such things, and be free of them. Don't forget to give thanks, there is so much to be thankful for! Then, ahhhh. Peace. Fix your eyes on all things good and praiseworthy... peace.

Helen Lemmel long ago wrote a hymn with this refrain:

> Turn your eyes upon Jesus,
> Look full in his wonderful face,
> And the things of earth will grow strangely dim,
> In the light of his glory and grace.

If you would live life rich and full, you have to learn to choose light. There is a turning – a turning from shadow to sunshine, a turning of your eyes from the things that are tattered and torn, the things that are painful and bleak, to the one surefire source of all that is good, all that is love, all that is hope: Jesus.

The Bible never negates that life is onerous, heartbreaking, grinding; it simply says to fix your eyes on what is not.

In every bout of depression I have suffered, there has been a moment when I have chosen darkness. There has been a moment of clarity, a moment of decision: I will step off of this precipice, I will give in to the hypnotic pull of despair. For me, it is similar to the decision one makes to call in sick – you dial the phone, you tell the boss, you hang up and sigh with relief, sink into the pillow, dim the lights, shut out the world. Leave me alone, I am sick. There are moments when darkness has all the appeal of a nice long nap. Light, like getting out of bed, takes energy.

If you would not go down that road, the months of sadness like a bad case of pneumonia, you had better learn to pay attention to that moment of choice. Grab hold of your weary heart and pull hard, throw your weight into it – Do. Not. Lie. Down. Get up! Choose now, this moment, choose light, defy the darkness and the sinking into shadow. Name your blessings, holler them out loud. I am thankful for the color of the sky behind the tree outside my window! I am thankful for coffee! I am thankful for the time we danced in the park!

Remember, you silly Israelite, remember what the Lord has done. Do not gaze in dismay at the desert you wander in, remember the Red Sea. Remember the Passover. Remember the burning bush.

Don't tell me your troubles today. I am sure they are real and not imagined. I am sure the road is long. But don't tell me you are weary, tell me about the time God answered your prayer, tell me about the color of your baby's eyes, tell me about your very favorite flavor of cheesecake, and maybe I'll go out and buy you a slice. Your list of heartaches is dark and deadly. Scribble out instead a list of praise.

'Do not go gentle into that good night... Rage, rage, against the dying of the light,' shouted Dylan Thomas, and I am in a shouting mood today. Choose light! Choose joy! Spend your last gasp of energy and pounce on it, don't let go.

I thank you God for sunny days!

I thank you God for rain!

I thank you for laughter, and for tears, for the fierce will to fight and the gift of rest. I thank you for King of the Mountain Joy. I thank you for your suffering. I thank you for constellations, for six-sided snowflakes, for the inexplicable duckbilled platypus and that ridiculous thing my husband does when he loads the dishwasher that always drives me crazy – because at least we have a dishwasher and we have each other and when I collapse in a fury of tears there is a friend to hug who'll kiss my hair.

Rage, rage, against the dying of the light! Shine your way glorious into the night and scar it forever with the dazzle-bright light of hope. Satan, that cave troll, hates light, and he will shrink away. He must.

Choose hope, even when hope hurts, and hope will let the light in. Or if you have no courage left to hope, give thanks for what has already come. Thanksgiving, says the wise Ann Voskamp, always precedes the miracle.

If you have no words to give thanks, borrow some.

This is my Father's world,
He shines in all that's fair.
In the rustling grass I hear Him pass,
He speaks to me everywhere.
This is my Father's world,
Oh let me ne'er forget
That though the wrong seems oft so strong,
God is the ruler yet.

Maltbie Davenport Babcock

You may struggle with depression, and even after making a commitment to give thanks, the struggle may dog you still. Your serotonin might be chronically low, your anxiety levels ramped too high. I would never wish to add to your worries the fear that you just aren't thankful enough. Many of the most honorable men in history have been plagued by depression – William Cowper, Charles Spurgeon, Abraham Lincoln, and Martin Lloyd-Jones, to name a few. The percentage of artists and writers who've suffered from depression is off the charts. There is some mysterious link between melancholy and creativity; some truly extraordinary people are just predisposed to it, for no fault of their own. 'But why was the man blind from birth?' they asked Jesus. 'His own sin, or his parents'?' Neither, answered the Lord. But for the inscrutable purposes of God, that He might through this struggle be glorified.

So I don't say that the dark night of the soul is a sin. What I am suggesting is that a deeply thankful life is a balm for weary souls, like hot tea to banish January's chill.

My own struggle with depression is always magnified in the gray days of winter. The doctor told me recently that I should buy a lamp specially made for those with Seasonal Affective Disorder. Sunlight combats depression, and plugging in the next best thing can help alleviate the blues. Choosing light in a spiritual sense is the same thing – kindling a flame to drive away shadows.

One of the most incredible facts about life in Christ is that we are offered peace and joy quite independently of our circumstances. Paul writes of joy from a prison cell, Jesus speaks of peace on His way to the cross. Although Christians are often called Pollyannas, Christianity is lived out in the trenches of sacrifice and suffering. Sounds gloomy, but there is hope here – a secret well of joy Satan cannot touch, bellow and bluster all he may. Still, it can be terribly hard to remember to choose light on dark days, awfully hard to fix our eyes on Jesus when the waves crash. It's much easier to latch on to a tangible substitute: this person makes me happy, this place is kinda nice. I'm like a dopey little bird who keeps trying to build nests in the middle of a logging camp. Oops, my tree just got chopped down, try again. Uh-oh, nest #14 demolished, try again. This is not my home, but I keep trying to set up housekeeping here, keep forgetting that Jesus is my treasure and heaven my home. Pin my hopes on a tottering tree and my nest is doomed.

***

When my husband and I, blessed beyond measure, were given the opportunity to take a sabbatical we retreated for several months from the stresses of ministry and the weary world. We withdrew to a mountain to spend time with Jesus. It seemed like it would last forever. But the day came when we had to return.

We stood at the top of the hill, at the particular bend in the road where we always turned around, pivoted in the mud, and stood rooted in it, our boots sinking in with stubbornness: here is where we will stay. The sun was setting in a rush; already the shadows rose up from the cliff bottoms to the east, and the tops, still sunbathing, faded fast. Only the really big mountain to the south was still clearly hanging on to daylight. It was time to go.

If peace were a place, this would be it. Peace, where aspen grow to unbelievable size. Peace, where red-winged blackbirds, misreading the calendar, sing spring through the snow. Peace, in a snug cabin stocked with board games and popcorn, stuck in another century. In Peace, you have time to pause at the window and notice things. You see a bird, a pretty one, maybe a bluebird, and you think, now what is the point of that bird? It doesn't contribute anything practical to the world; it just sings a bit, and really, what good is such a small song? And you stand there, idle, with the dishcloth just dangling, and listen, and it is so quiet that that bird is all that you hear, that flash of sapphire against the snow is all that you see, and you wonder what kind of logic rules a world where singing sapphires flit through the trees going their happy-go-lucky way for no practical purpose. And then you are thinking about who would dream up such a world, full of flashes of beauty and grace, but where, time to time, one of those same bright birds crashes into a window and dies, and who would notice? And you are thinking deep theological thoughts, all because it was quiet and still, and you were paying just a tiny bit of attention.

I like Peace. I was not in favor of leaving. And so I stood in the twilight, begging the day to rewind, willing time to stretch out long and lazy like a cat. And it began to dawn on me that if Peace is a place, I would be leaving the next day, heading back down the mountain to the rushing world below. Sirens and miscreants, hurry and worry, jangle and rattle and hum. But if I was somehow, still, listening – if I could manage to pay a tiny bit of attention, maybe I would spot the city bluebirds. Maybe, if Peace is not a place but a person, Peace could come home with me.

We left the mountain, came back to civilization. We drove through a minor blizzard on a long and tipsy highway, clutching the wheel and breathing deep. We added two hours to our trip via a not-optional detour – the pass was closed – arriving tired and frazzled. Back in the world of TV and Internet, we learned immediately of a demoralizing act of senseless violence, exactly where we were heading. I wanted to turn around, back through the blizzard, back to my happy place. But Peace was with me, and (no doubt with a longsuffering sigh) patted my hand in an *easy there* way.

Find quiet, Kate. Turn off the noisemakers. Be still. Pay attention. God is alive and well in the city, too. Look for Him. Slow down. Choose light, the Light of the World. Spend time with Him today. Remember all He has done. He is Peace.

10: Rest

If there is no Sabbath – no regular and commanded not-working, not-talking – we soon become totally absorbed in what we are doing and saying, and God's work is either forgotten or marginalized. When we work we are most god-like, which means that it is in our work that it is easiest to develop god-pretensions. Un-sabbathed, our work becomes the entire context in which we define our lives. We lose God-consciousness, God-awareness, sightings of resurrection. We lose the capacity to sing "This is my Father's world" and end up chirping little self-centered ditties about what we are doing and feeling.

Eugene Peterson[1]

1. Eugene Peterson, *Christ Plays in Ten Thousand Places* (Grand Rapids: W.B Eerdmans Publishing Co., 2005), 117.

It was about three o'clock in the morning, and the baby was yowling. He'd been fed, changed, burped, swaddled, snuggled, rocked and kissed, and he would not stop crying. I was a new mom, young, enthusiastic, *exhausted*. This business of giving up my eight hour beauty sleep was not sitting well with me. I wondered how I could ever keep it up, how I could joyfully take care of responsibilities with a permanently fogged brain and sluggish steps, how I could give a single ounce more to this utterly dependent creature who'd drunk me dry. A wave of anger swept over me as I looked at the tiny, red-faced screecher, and I thought *this is why people shake their babies.* Suddenly I was afraid, afraid of my own lack of self-control, afraid of this ugly anger. I laid the little howler in the crib and turned my back, walked across the little garret room, and knelt down. I couldn't trust myself to love this baby at the moment. I needed to pray. A few minutes passed, my son still wailing. My husband stumbled into the room. 'What – why is he crying? Did you feed him? What are you doing?' He took in the baby, abandoned in his crib, and me, kneeling on the floor. 'Oh...' And he took over, sent me back to bed, scooped the bundle and gave love. For me, rest.

Ministry is not so different, or the Christian life in general, for that matter. I give, I serve, I dry out, get weary. What I desperately need is rest. Some kind of pioneer instinct won't let me sit down, sit still, loiter. *Just keep swimming, swimming, swimming,* I mutter, and press on. But Jesus never intended us to stagger under impossible loads, never delegated the weight of the world to us. Rest, He says. Rest.

It has always seemed curious to me that as a culture, we uphold the Ten Commandments – no idols, no adultery, no murder – but disregard

Number Four,
the Sabbath's for
our worship and for rest.

Sabbath-keeping rest, given by God on Week One, seems a relic, not pertinent in our computer age. We toss it out along with the levitical purification rites and dietary regulations, some kind of Old Testament throw-back, with a purpose as outdated as unleavened bread baked on coals. Jesus blasts the Pharisees for their Sabbath-keeping zealotry and we throw the baby right out the back door along with the tub of filthy bathwater. Pharisees, bad, Sabbath, bad.

But what if Sabbath is a gift, not a burden? What if rest is just that, rest, ceasing from striving? Enjoying the fruit that sprouted on the tree during the long work week? Why would we turn that down?

The precious invitation stands: 'Come to me, all who labor and are heavy laden, and I will give you rest. Take my yoke upon you, and learn from me, for I am gentle and lowly in heart, and you will find rest for your souls. For my yoke is easy, and my burden is light.'[2]

---

2. Matthew 11:28-30

Rest implies hard work. The first Sabbath fell on the heels of six days of creation. The Word sang the world into existence, kindled a million million stars, established boundaries for the sea, designed photosynthesis, cultivated a fantastic garden, molded ten thousand species out of clay, blew into man the breath of life and officiated a wedding. It was a long week. From the beginning, God created human beings for work – not the dismal work that we inherited from the fall, but creative, joyful, rewarding work. Adam's first task was poetry – naming the wild profusion of strange and exotic animals. His first office was Eden, and his responsibility? Running the world, more or less – participating with God in the establishment of civilization.

The Sabbath was instituted before thorns and thistles invaded the ground, pre-tragedy. The Sabbath was necessary even in perfection, a day of rest. This puzzles and enchants me. Why rest if work is play? Why rest if work is delight? Perhaps not for the toll work takes on the body, but for the opportunity it affords for reflection, and for worship. Adam had the incredible chance to partner with Adonai, Lord of all creation, and even the work was worship. Can you even begin to grasp what life would be like in constant friendly conversation with God?

But we can't imagine that, because we live in a brier patch that came courtesy of doubt and greed. Our work, though it retains a dignified echo of Eden, is hampered by difficulty, frustration, and futility. How much more important is rest now?

God seems to have a work hard, play hard ethic here, in which rest is no shame, but built-in. It allows for reflection, for conversation with God, and now, in a fallen world, for recuperation. And so, rest also implies getting back to work. If you would continue at a world-changing pace, you'll have to rest.

Refusing rest greatly reduces your shelf-life in service. You just can't keep going at a breakneck pace forever. Spiritual battle is intense, wounds are inevitable. For Navy Seals, mandatory rest follows any tour of duty. So it is for Christians. Weekly, rest comes in the form of Sabbath. And sometimes, after a long season of service, rest comes in the form of sabbatical.

Rest delivers us from self-importance. Refusing rest is just pride, pure and simple. 'I am Wonder Woman!' we cry, 'I am Super Man!' But we court burnout; we invite the enemy to wear us out. He doesn't need coaxing. He'd be delighted to destroy us, and in the process make us bitter and resentful. Unrest is a recipe for a rancid heart.

Refusing to rest often betrays a mentality that esteems your own importance at highly vaulted levels. I can't rest, you say. How would the world go on without me? Surprisingly, the world can go on just fine. Whatever is urgent can wait while you recharge. Or is the issue money? God can provide for your needs even if you take Sundays off. (Here's a little secret: God is big enough to handle the consequences of your obedience. Perhaps He took them into account when He set up the system in the first place). Rest is built-in to the yoke we are called to carry; to try to pull the ox-cart without accepting the relief of rest is to take on more than we were meant to bear.

In the context of the church, rest for workers delivers us from the 80-20 rule, that axiom of the long-suffering 20 per cent who do 80 per cent of the work. Allowing the 20 to pace themselves insures that at least some of the 80 step up. How can they when the 20 won't step back? Why should they?

Refusing rest is often a refusal to delegate, if not for pride, for fear (*what disaster befalls those who relax?*), for simplicity (*I'll just do it myself, it's easier than finding a volunteer*), or for lack of imagination. But sharing the workload is kindness, both for the weary and for the shy, too timid to offer help. Because this work, soul work, if carried out at the pace God intended, is a joy to do. If it isn't life-giving, something – in quantity or in quality – is amiss.

I once heard a fable about a man who was given by God a small, smooth stone to carry on his journey. Along the way, he was stopped by many friends, who asked if he would carry their stones as well, until, finally, staggering under a giant pile of rocks, he fell exhausted by the roadside and cried out to God. 'Why did you give me such a burden to bear?' he lamented. And of course, the simple answer came. 'I did not ask you to carry these. You took this burden upon yourself.'

If it is silly to take on more than we were meant to, it's just plain stupid to try to out-do Jesus.

Dallas Willard points out that we cannot hope to live like Jesus at a moment of crisis if we do not live as Jesus lived day in and day out. And how did Jesus live? After a forty day fast,

> ...he was alone much of the time, often spending the entire night in solitude and prayer before serving the needs of his disciples and hearers the following day.
>
> Out of such preparation, Jesus was able to lead a public life of service through teaching and healing. He was able to love his closest companions to the end – even though they often disappointed him greatly and seemed incapable of entering into his faith and works. And then he was able to die a death unsurpassed for its intrinsic beauty and historical effect.
>
> And in this truth lies the secret of the easy yoke: the secret involves living as he lived in the entirety of his life – adopting his overall life-style.... The general human failing is to want what is right and important, but at the same time not to commit to the kind of life that will produce the action we know to be right and the condition we want to enjoy.[3]

Jesus' lifestyle of spiritual discipline, including Sabbath, times of silence, and regular, rigorous prayer, sustained His lifestyle of service and sacrifice. Hadn't we better commit to this ourselves?

Rest allows for stillness, and in stillness we rediscover wonder. This week, as the forecast

---

3. Dallas Willard, *The Spirit of the Disciplines.* (New York: HarperSanFransisco, 1988), 5-6.

predicted copious piles of snow for Colorado, my small son and I read a book about the weather. Outside, the sky grew dense and white, and we, warm and toasty inside, read about cirrus clouds, fog, snowflakes. Of course you will know about snowflakes, that each one is different, yet most are hexagons, that the Inuit have over 100 words for snow, including 'auviq' (good for igloos) and 'piqsig' (the blowing kind). You will have waded out in it as a child, made a snow angel, a raisin-eyed man with soggy scarf, you will have memories of sledding and snowball fights. But when was the last time it amazed you? If Michelangelo painstakingly snipped a million paper snowflakes – perfect, unique, 10 to the top of an eraser, and you were allowed to stand among them swirling, would you marvel?

Psalm 19, a psalm for daybreak, for daily praise, announces: 'The heavens declare the glory of God, and the sky above proclaims his handiwork. Day to day pours out speech, and night to night reveals knowledge.' Poured out of the sky above, every snowflake is a written call to astonishment – how beautiful is the Lord! How endlessly creative! How infinitely painstaking! If I were to number His thoughts, I would run out of numbers. If I could count His gifts, my voice would grow hoarse and dim. Upon the wicked and the righteous He pours out beauty, upon the mindful and the oblivious He lavishes grace.

We had an appointment at the orthodontist; on the way home it began to snow. Swish, swish. With a quick flick of the wrist I pulled a lever and the wipers sprang to life, with every pass obliterating a thousand works of art. How could I see them? I was not still.

'Wonder' gets a bad rap. It's a Pollyanna word, a little-orphan-Annie-in-Daddy-Warbucks'-mansion word. It's a word for dreamy pop singers and inspirational posters. It's a word, I think, for anyone with eyes to see.

Anne Lamott writes, 'This is our goal as writers, I think; to help others have this sense of – please forgive me – wonder, of seeing things anew, things that can catch us off guard, that break in on our small, bordered worlds. When this happens, everything feels more spacious. Try walking around with a child who's going, "Wow, wow! Look at that dirty dog! Look at that burned-down house! Look at that red sky!" And the child points and you look, and you see, and you start going, "Wow! Look at that huge crazy hedge! Look at that teeny little baby! Look at the scary dark cloud!" I think this is how we are supposed to be in the world – present and in awe.'[4]

In awe – of what? If you live, as I do, in a sizable city, you are in an enviable position for wonder. This is a fact I have had a hard time warming up to, but it's true. God's crowning creation, after all, was not the ridiculously intricate flagellum (with

---

4. Anne Lamott, *Bird by Bird*. (New York: Random House, 1994), 98.

its rotor, driveshaft, and propeller)[5] , nor was it the sun setting rosy over the Grand Canyon, nor even the bright clouds of the Milky Way. *'Very good'* He reserved for Adam and Eve.

The nearest notable intersection to our neighborhood is the juncture of Havana and Alameda: eight lanes, including turn lanes, run north-south and six east-west. Cars pile up six deep per lane at a red light. Beside me I might spot a defiant teenager (foster care? drugs in the house?) or a lonely wife (husband deployed? colicky baby?) I tap the steering wheel while someone tears past on the way to the hospital, while another slowly edges towards the cemetery. One hundred cars? Three hundred passengers? Three hundred occasions for awe? In the backseat my children laugh. What is a human being, that we laugh? Can biology (or only theology) account for glee? Their strong hearts pump gallons of rich red blood cells, untiring, untaught.

Chat with a group of friends. Someone will tell of a remarkable string of coincidences. These ripple out to profoundly affect a dozen people, whose reactions spin out to affect a dozen dozen more. Who is orchestrating this symphony of dominoes? How complicated are these harmonies? Creation

---

5. The flagellum is a whip-like structure found in many micro-organisms. It acts as a tiny propeller and is invisible to the naked eye. It is incredibly intricate and complex. Biochemistry professor Michael Behe has used this microscopic organelle to illustrate his argument for 'irreducible complexity,' the notion that an organism's interdependent parts defy evolutionary theory and are proof of design.

might have begun with a six-day process celebrated on the seventh day, but it continues moment by moment in a billion particularities around the globe. Only the *ex nihilo* bit – out of nothing – is finished (and even that – who am I to say He doesn't go on creating elsewhere?) Souls are born and other souls born again; each spring the woods dazzle with new life; miracles of serendipity bloom all around. The wonder appropriate in Eden is new every morning.

Eugene Peterson maintains that 'Wonder is the only adequate launching pad for exploring a spirituality of creation, keeping us open-eyed, expectant, alive to life that is always more than we can account for, that always exceeds our calculations, that is always beyond anything we can make.'[6] Alive to life... aware, available to see, awake from fingertip to cochlea, *alive*, like a kid on a roller coaster, like a shepherd startled witless by the announcement of angels. Life is bursting all around; are we alive to life?

But who has time for wonder? Who, in the crush of time – tick, tock, don't stop, I'm late! I'm late! I'm late! – can pause to observe the grand drama unfolding all around? None of us would presume to burst into the Kennedy Center mid-concerto and stomp through hollering. Well, maybe my children might. But most of us would, I hope, gently crack the door, whisper, tiptoe, find a nearby seat, sit a spell. And yet we routinely crash through God's

---

6. Eugene Peterson, *Christ Plays in Ten Thousand Places*. (Grand Rapids: Wm. B. Eerdmans Publishing, 2005), 52.

creation, oblivious. What a lack of awe. What a lack of... respect.

Stillness is the right response to mystery, and stillness can only be achieved when we set down our work and look around. 'Be still, and know that I am God.'

A daily moment of stillness, or better yet, regular pauses throughout the day, invite me to look up, give thanks, reset my heart. Moments of rest let me step for a moment into a quiet chapel, kneel for a moment while the world rushes by, and notice Jesus. I have to stake out margins in my life – room to allow for a change of plans, room to face setbacks without panic, room to breathe. I'm only able to have moments of stillness if I plan for them.

A rhythm of weekly Sabbath dedicates an entire day to the discipline of stillness. An entire day of prayer, worship, reflection, taking time to enjoy loved ones – this is the weekly reset button that makes the work week worthwhile.

Rest reminds us that this world is not all there is; we are sojourners traveling home.

There is an achingly beautiful, spare little poem written several thousand years ago: perhaps you know it. 'The Lord is my shepherd,' it begins, best-loved psalm of the shepherd-king.

Did David stand gazing from a palace window as he wrote these words? Did he shrug off his bodyguards and go for a long walk outside the city walls? After all of the battles, all of the upheaval of his political life, did he regret the loss of days spent on a hillside, tending flocks? He could surely remember: green grass, cool shade, frisky lambs, sunsets, quiet. Psalm 23 is David's ode to the giver of stillness and rest. His memory calls across the ages, inviting us. Come, traveler, rest your bones.

> The Lord is my shepherd; I shall not want.
> He makes me lie down in green pastures.
> He leads me beside still waters.
> He restores my soul.
> He leads me in paths of righteousness
> For his name's sake.
> Even though I walk through the valley of the shadow of death,
> I fear no evil, for you are with me;
> your rod and your staff, they comfort me.
> You prepare a table before me in the presence of my enemies;
> you anoint my head with oil;
> My cup overflows.
> Surely goodness and mercy shall follow me all the days of my life,
> And I shall dwell in the house of the Lord forever.

Here's a psalm with rare power to illuminate and define our lives. C.S. Lewis wrote, 'I believe in Christianity as I believe that the sun has risen: not only because I see it, but because by it I see everything else.' I might say the same of this Psalm: 'I believe in Psalm 23 as I believe that the sun has risen: not only because I see it, but because by it I see everything else.' By its light, I see a long and dusty road, a fence running along beside, and finally, a gate up ahead. And by the gate is a familiar person – not familiar because I have seen His face before, but familiar like something risen up out of a recurring dream. He is far off, but I can see that He is smiling; He waves. I hear my own name called out in a jovial, hearty greeting. Though my back and feet are aching, and the pack I carry is heavy, I catch a second wind. I begin to run. And then I'm home, dropping my burden, crying with relief; the man, in His rough clothes, is folding me into an embrace. His eyes – His eyes are so bright, so kind, so joyful – no far-off, glaring God, but Love in a shepherd's face. And He holds open the gate, ushers me in. This pasture is no muddy cow-paddy, it is beauty, from the velvet grass to the towering trees, the sapphire streams, the rolling purple mountains in the distance. I see grace, rest, freedom from fear. I see that I will never hunger nor thirst again. I see companionship, tender care, restoration and healing.

Like David, we rest. We allow the shepherd to lead us to water, and consent to drink. We lay down our burdens for a moment (someday for eternity) and recline on the verdant grass. We remember where in the green world we are heading, and who is waiting to welcome us home.

11: Unhooked and Unhindered

Therefore, since we are surrounded by such a great cloud of witnesses, let us throw off everything that hinders and the sin that so easily entangles, and let us run with perseverance the race marked out for us. Let us fix our eyes on Jesus, the author and perfecter of our faith, who for the joy set before him endured the cross, scorning its shame, and sat down at the right hand of the throne of God. Consider him who endured such opposition from sinful men, so that you will not grow weary and lose heart.

Hebrews 12:1-3 (NIV)

Inordinate care for the present life, and fondness for it, is a dead weight upon the soul, that pulls it down when it would ascend upward, and pulls it back when it should press forward; it makes duty and difficulties harder and heavier than they would be.

Matthew Henry[1]

I have always loved a good puzzle. Jigsaws, logical conundrums, little wooden boxes with hidden springs that pop open... I love them all. And the Bible is chock full of enough little mysteries to keep Nancy Drew busy for a lifetime. One of the chief ways this is true is the plethora of paradoxes.

> Jesus is fully man AND fully God.

> The Lord our God, the Lord is one... Father, Son and Holy Spirit.

> Honor your father and mother; hate your father and mother. (Exod. 20:12; Luke 14:26)

> Jesus is the Prince of Peace, who came to bring a sword. (Isa. 9:6; Matt. 10:34)

Each of the Biblical paradoxes forces us to pause, circle back, dig a little deeper. Each, like a little wooden box with a hidden spring, holds the power to pop open, to surprise and delight. If you read the Bible through from Genesis to Revelation, you might miss them, because Part I of the puzzle might be stated in 2 Kings and Part II in 1 Corinthians,

---

1. Henry, Matthew. *An Exposition of the Old and New Testament volume 6* (Philadelphia: Haswell, Barrington and Haswell, 1838), p. 749

a thousand pages apart. But if you mix up your reading and juxtapose odd bits of Old and New Testament, sometimes you'll come across one you've never noticed before. Here's a favorite of mine.

In Luke 12, Jesus tells the story of a rich landowner, who has a vexing lack of room in his barns for all of his crops. 'Here's what I'll do,' thinks he, 'build bigger barns!' Satisfied, he congratulates himself for his wealth and kicks back to relax. 'Now I can take it easy,' he says, 'eat, drink, and be merry.'

But God is not happy with Rich Guy. 'You fool!' He thunders. 'Time's up. Tonight you die. What good are your big barns now?'

It is a familiar warning, and so often repeated that 'eat, drink, and be merry' is shorthand for folly. It brings to mind the Romans, lounging half-dressed in their steaming baths right up until the collapse of their empire – unprepared, vain, reality-TV bubble-heads.

So what to make of Ecclesiastes? After a long list of his meaningless projects and misspent priorities, the wise old king concludes, 'I know that there is nothing better for men than to be happy and do good while they live. That everyone may eat and drink, and find satisfaction in all his toil – this is the gift of God' (Eccles. 3:12-13, NIV).

And there's the puzzle. What can it mean? Using almost identical language, Jesus condemns the wealthy landowner for his desire to 'eat, drink and be merry,' while Solomon recommends that we do just that. I think that wrapped inside this paradox is a great secret, the answer of how to experience an abundant life while aliens and strangers in the world.

Meet Joe and Bob. Joe is a millionaire. Early on in life, he wrote out a detailed list of goals. 'I will retire at age thirty. I will own five luxury cars. I will sail around the world on a yacht. I will send my children to Ivy League schools. I will buy my wife diamonds every year on our anniversary.' Yada, yada, yada. Joe worked hard, ruthless in his pursuit of these goals, and one by one he checked them off his life list. He dreamed big, and backed up from the desired outcomes to outline the necessary steps to achieve each one. Joe will tell you that if you dream it, you can do it, but it takes elbow grease. Joe will tell you to never compromise on your goals, and to be willing to make sacrifices to get there. And after he's had a few drinks, Joe might just tell you that his success is empty, his relationships bankrupt, and his fears debilitating.

Bob, on the other hand, is the picture of joy. His house is snug and cozy, his finances steady but unremarkable, his relationships glowing. Bob loves nothing more than a big, merry feast with his friends and family, a warm evening of laughter and games. Bob, too, has pursued a list of life goals with determination, but his goals were a little different. 'I will learn what it means to love God with all of my heart, soul, mind and strength. I will work hard to love my neighbor as myself. I will fix my eyes on Jesus, and run with perseverance to finish strong. I will find out what Jesus meant when He said that He came to give me life to the full. I will live for an audience of

One.' Bob will tell you that life is an adventure, that Jesus is his best friend, that he can't wait to go Home.

Joe's happiness is entirely hooked into the value system of the world, because in his mind, this is all there is. He has already reached the pinnacle of success and has nothing to look forward to. Frankly, he's bored. He congratulates himself for his achievement, and evaluates himself according to his accomplishments, yet lives with nagging guilt. After all, he's broken a lot of promises, told some outrageous lies, and stepped on folks to get where he is. He lives for himself, but sabotages his own relationships to stay at the top. He trusts no one, because the people in his life are envious, grasping, and insincere. On the other hand, he desperately craves others' approval (though he'd never admit it).

Bob is unhooked, unhindered, and free. He does not care about the world's value system, and doesn't regard that he owns anything himself anyway. He doesn't have much, so he's got nothing to lose. Bob is always up for an adventure, and gets a kick out of the twists and turns his life has taken following God. He expects the unexpected. Bob receives everything in his life as a gift, as grace. He is constantly amazed by God's generosity, and humbly concedes he doesn't deserve anything. He delights in God's forgiveness, and keeps a clean slate. He loves freely, extending to others the grace he's received from God. On the other hand, he doesn't much mind what other people think of him, because he looks to God for the kind of unconditional love other people can never give.

So he's an honest guy; he'll tell you what he really thinks. He consults God when he makes plans and doesn't care whether you approve. Bob is fearless, bold, and confident.

Either one, Bob or Joe, could proclaim 'Eat, drink, and be merry, for tomorrow you may die.' But Bob lives in hope of heaven every day; Joe lives in fear of hell.

***

One day, ordinary in the beginning, I will at last go home. I will pay my last bill, eat my last meal, hug my last hug. I will say goodbye to the old earth and see a world untainted by sin, unpolluted and perfect. I will meet Jesus face to face. I have often wondered about that moment – what will He say? How will I answer? Will He ask me hard questions like the landowners in His parables? *How's the crop? Where did you invest?* Will He hit play on the movie of my life and review it under my squirming gaze? Often I think of the kinds of accountability questions we ask each other here, and picture Jesus as judge, or professor. But there is another kind of question He might ask.

I came that you might have life, and have it to the full, He might say. *It was for freedom that I set you free. How'd that go?*

What would it look like to live full, to live free? How might a person's life be transformed by joy? What would it look like to really understand that you are fully loved, uniquely created, and designed for a purpose, and to live a life abandoned to the will of God?

A full life, a free life, is rested – not rushed, trusting – not anxious, thankful – not grasping. It's a rocking chair on the front porch, a walk in the woods, a juicy peach, tickling the kids. It's a long soak in Psalms, prayer that's conversation, and a good laugh. A full heart is unhooked from the things of the world – unhooked from fear, unhooked from busyness, unhooked from disappointment. A free heart is unhindered, unobstructed, unbound. And it really doesn't give a hoot what anyone else thinks.

Jesus, I would like to be able to answer, *You were my best friend. You taught me to have deep-rooted joy, childlike faith, great love. Life with You was always an adventure. You blessed me far beyond anything I could have ever asked for or imagined. You filled my heart to overflowing, and You set me free.*

***

Paul was a man who could answer like that. By the tail end of Acts, Paul, on house arrest, awaits execution in a Roman rental house on permanent lock-down. Luke describes him thus: 'preaching the kingdom of God, and teaching concerning the Lord Jesus Christ with all openness, unhindered.' (Acts 28:31, NASB) Unhindered? But he's been arrested! And yet he is absolutely free in all the ways that matter. Paul is unhooked from the love of stuff, unhindered by sin, unconcerned with people's good opinion of him, and not bothered by fear. He's not frantically busy, not anxious, and not weighed down by condemnation. As a result, he can approach the throne of grace with confidence; Jesus has called him 'friend.'

Free from Stuff

Paul is free from the tyranny of envy and from enslavement to his possessions, because he considers 'everything as loss because of the surpassing worth of knowing Christ' (Phil. 3:8). Stuff just isn't important to him.

We understood this so much better after our sabbatical break from civilization. There was something about packing for a five-month trip that really brought home the big truths about life: I do not need that many shirts. I have bottles of cardamom, turmeric, and coriander that I have used maybe once but that have been occupying space in my little cabinet for a whole lotta years. And I really do not plan to ever re-watch all of those DVDs – DVD players are on the brink of extinction anyway.

What do you need when you're leaving for five months on a cross-country trip? What's really, really essential? Because whatever you pack you have to lug – in and out of cabins and cottages, in and out of snow, rain, 100-degree days. Whatever you pack you have to sit on, under, or crammed between as you head down the interstate – you'd better like it if it's going to be poking you in the ribs for days on end. And what, when you've not needed it or missed it for five months, do you really need at all?

We threw things out on the way, outgrown clothes (and yes, in five months, the kids outgrew a lot), holey jeans. We lost a one-eyed stuffed Tiger that turned out to be super-important after all – the whole family cried along with Little Man – and witnessed together the miracle when it turned up in a Pennsylvania hotel and got Fed-Exed back to us. We learned that you can spend hours with the same crate of Legos and make something new every day, that long walks are better than Yahoo, and that the same thirty recipes over and over seems like more variety than what I produce with shelves of cook books.

We stayed in places beautiful and places dumpy, lived in others' houses and saw what they treasured. We learned what we didn't miss, to our great astonishment. We didn't miss TV. We didn't miss the Internet. We did miss some books, our laundry room!, the grill.

We came home, looked with new eyes. We did some sorting, separating, paring down. If it can't fit in the back of the Dodge Durango, maybe it's not so necessary after all.

This little realization has been incredibly freeing. It opens up huge vistas of possibility: we could move anywhere! We could give up anything! Things that we have always paid for – out of habit, out of social pressure – are things we can live without; giving them up allows us to spend money, or give money, to what is more important.

Free from Sin

Paul is also unhampered by sin. No compulsive sin issues threaten to tear apart his life or jeopardize his reputation; the Spirit has set him free from the law of sin and death.[2] His soul is a still pond, unruffled,

---

2.   Romans 8:2

because 'the mind governed by the Spirit is life and peace.'[3]

Sin is sticky stuff. It ensnares us, forcing us to harden our hearts against God and sin still more to avoid being found out. When finally we want out, we have to backtrack along the trail of damage we've created and confess the mess we've made. Not fun. I'm convinced that concern for personal holiness is critical if you don't want to experience life as a self-made prison.

The writer of Hebrews gives the brilliant word picture of an athlete, streamlined and efficient, throwing aside anything that might slow him down, specifically any sin. I think of swimmers, every hair shaved, swimsuit as minimal and clingy as possible, slicing through water like butter. Sin for a Christian is like a big pair of hiking boots when you're doing the breast stroke, waterlogged and heavy. And yet we live in a world which justifies, qualifies, extols, and promotes sin at every turn. It is easy to get sucked in, to purchase one by one a pile of the world's values and layer them on, big, bulky hindrances that they are. The more our pet sins resemble the world's, the easier they are to ignore. The more we flaunt them (in the name of authenticity, perhaps), the more they undercut our relationship with a holy God.

It is sooo freeing (there's that word again) to recognize that I can't yank on the oars and row my way to holiness, but I can let out the sail and catch

---

3.   Romans 8:6 (NIV)

a lift. When Paul instructs us to 'be ye being filled' by the Holy Spirit in Ephesians 5:18, it is akin to being filled as a sail with wind. We surrender to another power and let it propel us, we give up control to another force. It changes us, carries us. Asking God to fill us with His Spirit is stepping aside so that the One who already dwells in our hearts can take over. His power is perfect, His desire for holiness is never distracted or diverted by temptation, His ability to choose rightly is unerring. When we simply acknowledge His authority, He is always available to work through us and do beautifully what we could never on our own strength achieve. As Peter puts it, 'His divine power has granted to us all things that pertain to life and godliness, through the knowledge of Him who called us to His own glory and excellence, by which He has granted to us His precious and very great promises, so that through them you may become partakers of the divine nature, having escaped from the corruption that is in the world because of sinful desire.'[4] *All things...* holiness is not out of reach.

Live a holy life, and live free indeed. The Psalmist says, 'I run in the path of your commands, for you have set my heart free.'[5] Freedom from sin equals freedom to live from the heart, unhooked and unhindered.

Free from Fear

Paul is free from fear of death, because for him, 'to live is Christ and to die is gain.'[6] The most

---

4.   2 Peter 1:3-4

5.   Psalm 119:32 (NIV)

6.   Philippians 1:21

terrifying thing in the world is death – survey any people group in history and I think you will find a thousand superstitions that testify this is so. But in Christ, we have great courage, for hell has no victory and death has no sting. We know that life is short, but heaven is everlasting. Jesus' death destroyed the power of death, to 'deliver all those who through fear of death were subject to lifelong slavery.'[7] The fear of death is paralyzing and demoralizing. Freed from it, we are bold risk-takers; we have nothing to lose.

Paul is also free from fear of persecution, because he trusts that suffering for Christ will always result in his own sanctification and God's glory. Go ahead, torture me, he says gleefully. You'll only be earning reward for me in heaven.

Personally, I harbor a deep-seated fear of torture, and can only hope that Christ would give me supernatural grace or a quick beheading to keep me from disgracing Him entirely under threat of sharp objects. But I am learning more and more that my 'light and momentary afflictions' are always padded by mercy and purposefully redeemed by the grace of God. More and more, I can stand up under pain because Christ gives me courage.

'Consider him who endured from sinners such hostility against himself, so that you may not grow weary or fainthearted.'[8] My Jesus was brave. He bought my bravery. Up ahead I see the finish line,

---

7. Hebrews 2:15
8. Hebrews 12:3

the cheering crowds, the homecoming committee. I don't lose heart because I am going home.

Unhooking the sharp tentacles of fear from our hearts is possible because we fill the void with love. Love crowds out worry, replacing anxiety with deep faith in a great and tender God. Fearless, unflappable, we can face down the future with aplomb.

Free as a Child

Clearly Paul is way past caring what anyone else thinks of him; he is unashamed of the gospel. Boldly and without hindrance, he shares the love of God, so simply and powerfully that the world is forever changed. Furthermore, he is completely steadfast in the knowledge of how wide and long and high and deep is His Father's love – a love that fills him 'to the measure of all the fullness of God!'[9] Unconcerned with anyone's good opinion save Christ's, Paul lets the gospel go out unhindered.

I think it is this last truth that is the key to freedom in Christ. Understanding God's love and my unshakable position as His child confers to me untouchable confidence and a great sigh of relief. My worth in His eyes is unassailable, my performance is irrelevant, and my personality is a God-given gift not in need of overhaul. I can let criticism roll off my back, I can make choices for an 'audience of One' and let the chips fall.

One of the most iconic photos ever taken in the Oval Office shows JFK working at his desk while

9. Ephesians 3:19 (NIV)

a curious little John Kennedy, Jr. plays underfoot, completely undaunted by the power or prestige of his father. What a picture! That's exactly how Christians can 'approach the throne of grace with confidence.' We are not interrupting an important dignitary's business meeting, we are drawing near our Abba. Secure in the love of God, we can carry on unceasing, conversational prayer.

I love Jesus' final words before the cross in the gospel of John. Jesus speaks of heaven, declares His love, calls us friends. He reminds the disciples that though they will certainly have trouble in this world, He has overcome the world. And tucked into some encouragement on the subject of prayer, Jesus says, 'Ask, and you will receive, that your joy may be full.... I do not say to you that I will ask the Father on your behalf; for the Father himself loves you, because you have loved me and have believed that I came from God.'[10] Chewing on this recently, I marveled. God doesn't answer my prayers to somehow please His Son, the member of the Trinity who really loves me; God loves to answer my prayers because God the Father loves me Himself. I am free to ask whatever I wish, just as my children can ask me for anything. *You want a Slurpee? I would love to give you a Slurpee! I just love to see you smile!*

Emboldened, I began to pray. What would you ask God for if you thought He might really answer? I was surprised by what poured out of my

---

10. John 16:24-27

uncensored heart. Not trying to couch my requests in spiritual lingo, I did not ask for the 'right' things. I didn't piously ask for wisdom or cleverly wish for more wishes. I found myself saying, 'Hey, this is who I think you made me to be. Can you help me to be that?' There were things I'd given up on praying for that I still really wanted; honestly, specifically, I listed them out. And the whole time, I felt God's presence, His warmth, and His great love.

For the next few weeks, I read on, out of John and into Acts. In Acts I saw a pattern; the disciples prayed, and then they were amazed. They prayed, and then they were amazed. I felt eager, tingly, ready to be amazed. And suddenly the answers began to pour in, one after another. God had heard my heart, and in love, He replied.

***

When Blaise Pascal met Christ, the experience so profoundly moved him that he wrote out an ecstatic account of it and sewed it into his breast pocket. For the rest of his life, next to his heart, he carried a reminder of fire, certitude, 'joy, joy, joy, tears of joy' and 'renunciation total and sweet.' He concluded with the words: 'Total submission to Jesus Christ and to my director. Eternally in bliss, in exchange for a day of hard training in this world. May I never forget your words.'

To truly know, experientially, the deep love of God, and the joy that comes of following Him, is to know with certitude where your true home is and Who your true Father is. It is to carry something in your heart with the power to utterly transform your life. The 'day of hard training' goes by in a blur with the promise of eternal bliss to look forward to. Armed with the love of God, you can live unhindered.

The world prizes freedom, worships independence but never tastes them. Harsh voices in our culture demand freedom as their due, at any expense; these same crusaders will never be released from guilt, fear, or resentment. Always struggling to measure up and never secure in their achievements, always stepping on someone else and never prepared for being stepped upon, always insisting on their absolute moral high ground and never quite able to forgive their own failures... Without Christ, freedom is a carnival attraction, a hall of mirrors, distorting, deceiving, and never delivering. In Christ, freedom is no excuse to indulge the sinful nature, but as Pascal put it, 'Total submission to Jesus Christ and to my director.' Freedom in Christ is an invitation to empty, so that, paradoxically, we may become full.

***

Out of my distress I called on the Lord;
the Lord answered me and set me free.
The Lord is on my side; I will not fear.
What can man do to me?[11]

Sabbatical came for me at a time when I felt stuck, like a motion-sick child strapped to a roller coaster and unable to get off. Many's the time I prayed

---

11. Psalm 118:5-6

in desperation for God to set me free. What I had in mind was a change in circumstance; what God offered was a change of heart. I expected, on sabbatical, that the change of pace would do me good, that the rest would refill me. I hoped that God would restore my trust (which I suspected was lacking) and reveal to me His love. Freedom, as such, wasn't something I knew I needed.

But here we are, months later, reveling in new, unanticipated freedom. I feel again a sense of excitement to see what God will do in and around me; instead of feeling trapped, I feel carried. I feel more certain of who I am and how I've been uniquely wired, and less obligated to be anyone else. I wear my cowboy boots and a grin, and I really don't care if you like them or not! I feel released from others' expectations, not because they've stopped expecting anything, but because I feel adored and cherished by my Father. What can man do to me? I feel unhooked from outcomes; daily I can obey, believing that God has given me exactly enough time to accomplish what matters most to Him, and let go of the pressure of results. If I have done my bit, He will use it however He wants. Bill Bright used to say, 'Success in witnessing is taking the initiative to share Christ in the power of the Holy Spirit and leaving the results to God.' Success in anything is like that – stepping out in faith and not worrying about the outcome.

What would it look like to live unhooked, unhindered? 'Joy, joy, joy, tears of joy.' May He write it on our hearts forever.

12: Home

I will arise and go now, and go to Innisfree,
And a small cabin build there, of clay and
*   wattles made:*
Nine beanrows will I have there, a hive for the
*   honey-bee;*
And live alone in the bee-loud glade.
And I shall have some peace there, for peace
*   comes dropping slow,*
Dropping from the veils of the morning to where
*   the cricket sings;*
There midnight's all a glimmer, and noon
*   a purple glow,*
And evening full of the linnet's wings.

I will arise and go now, for always night and day
I hear lake water lapping with low sounds by the
*   shore;*
While I stand on the roadway, or on the
*   pavements grey,*
I hear it in the deep heart's core.

W.B. Yeats[1]

I want to tell you about Home. I want to paint for you a picture so compelling that anything else pales in comparison, any less-than dream is exposed for the illusion it is. But it's a little tricky to tell you of a future I haven't seen any more than you have, a place I have never been. I could take you back, back to Eden, and tell you what we lost, so that you can begin to look forward to the restoration, but that too is a bit dicey.

> 'Where were you when I laid the foundation of the earth? Tell me, if you have understanding, who determined its measurements – surely you know! Or who stretched the line upon it? On what were its bases sunk, or who laid its cornerstone, when the morning stars sang together and all the sons of God shouted for joy? ...
>
> 'Where is the way to the dwelling of light, and where is the place of darkness?'[2]

I confess, I was not there; I did not hear that song. I cannot tell you, traveler, the way to the dwelling of light. The best I can do is study the One who sang

---

1. 'Lake Isle of Innisfree' 1888.

2. Job 38:4-7, 19

the song, study the One who is the light. What is Home like? It is the dwelling place of Love. How do you get there? Follow Him and find it.

If God is Love, then His dwelling place has been lovingly designed, no detail forgotten, as a gift of love. Home is joy, peace, unbroken friendship with God (friendship with God!) conversation, communion, walks in the garden. How is it possible? It has been so before; look at Eden.

If God's mercies are new every morning, then Home is tender. It is release from pain and struggle and want. It is presided over by the Healer, whose compassion never fails. Your wounds will be bandaged and balmed. Your heart will be restored, and you will find rest for your soul.

If God is grace, then Home is abundance. It is a place of feasting (the food is delicious!), reunion (laughter and embracing), celebration, victory, and consummation. *He brought me to his banqueting table, his banner over me is love.*

All equally share in this abundance; Christ is glorious over all and we, saints and sinners, are equally amazed. You may sit between jolly G.K. Chesterton and the formidable Jonathan Edwards and chat freely as a friend to each. You may have a gyro and baklava with Esther on Tuesday and a perfect plate of chimichangas with crazy Anne Lamott on Wednesday, all of you goggled by delight at this place you've landed, overwhelmed by love for your Savior. All of us got it wrong more often than we got it right, all of us know the scandal of forgiveness right down to our very bones.

If Christ is beauty, then Home is a sanctuary to loveliness. Imagine a place where the air is more clear, so that breathing it in you feel more awake, delighted by a thousand heady scents you've never smelled. We will move from blindness into sight, from fog to daylight, from deafness to hearing. All of your brain – the whole chunk that has lain dormant all your life – will awake. What will you think when at last you think clearly? What will you perceive when at last you can see?

If the Lord has been your dwelling place from generation to generation, then Home is, well, Home. It must be a place which feels at one and the same time completely familiar and extraordinarily *other,* more dazzling than the best of earth and more perfectly suited to you than your own living room. You, who have been your whole life an alien and a stranger, will step into your native country at last, and find that it exceeds your wildest expectations. After all, it is the place you were created to live, the place you've heard calling 'in the deep heart's core' all your life – that place you faintly remember dreaming about on a midsummer's night, that place you miss with a great ache when you're lonely or uncomfortable.

When I was a little girl my sister and I went to summer camp; one year my mother took advantage of our time away to do some projects around the house. She painted the walls, peeled up the old carpet, and swapped our bedrooms. Out with the old bedspreads – these were replaced by new ones we were allowed to choose before we left. When, after a week, we came home, we raced into the dear old house and up the stairs. There were our rooms, our beloved rooms, same as always, and yet different, fresher, spiffy. There were my favorite toys and belongings, there was my familiar bed, but all was bright and clean. I was home, and it was better than ever. How much more will Heaven feel like coming Home?

If Christ is creator, inventor, mathematician, artist, poet, and architect, then we, who will be like Him, will finally be unleashed. Home is where the great projects you never got to complete wait for you to dive in, where all you are can be brought to bear on epic tasks only you can accomplish, where your disabilities will blossom into great strengths, and you will emerge as from a cocoon into a new creature, glorious. You who were faithful in a Sunday school class may be given a university. You who were faithful with a canvas may be given the Sistine Chapel. Did you lead in the PTA? How about a city to govern? Did you tithe your paper boy salary? How about a million dollars? Did you lay on your back and dream castles in the clouds? How would you like to build that beauty in great marble blocks? As Randy Alcorn and others have pointed out, Adam and Eve were given work *before* the fall. Projects, stripped of sin and frustration, created with our personality and strengths in mind, are not onerous, but exhilarating. At Home, you will never be bored, but challenged, invigorated, and delighted.

Reading about, reflecting on, praying for, and aching for Home richly rewards all who dare spend an hour doing so. Remember Christmas Eve at about age eight? When you could barely sleep for the excitement? Let your homesick heart pine; don't stanch the longing. That very sorrow is a gift to lead you back to Christmas Eve. We were created for something higher, better, brighter than this sin-sick world, and when we allow ourselves to feel, we can begin to rise out of the muck and live with fresh hope.

When you desire something pure and perfect here on earth, recognize it for what it is, a signpost pointing you on your way. In itself, it cannot satisfy your soul. But does it reflect the love, creativity, holiness, and goodness of God? Look up, see perfection Himself, and worship.

You see fingerprints? Wonderful. Now press on, detective, and find the source of those prints. Don't get so caught up in the trace evidence that you forget the mystery.

**

It dangles there in front of me like a carrot on a stick, what I long for. All wholesome things – room for the kids to run and play, food fresh from the garden, air that smells faintly of orchards and hums with the lazy buzz of bumblebees. Land – a dream of hills, trees, distant mountains, crashing ocean, waterfalls, glimpses of shy creatures that dart into the safety of woods. Laughter, feasting, friendship, true companions, adventure. Home – I have strained to sketch it on graph paper since Mrs. Alred taught us how in the fourth grade, a house to contain all of the joys and comforts and warmth of fireplace, table, library, bed. When I was a kid, my designs included secret passageways, towers, elevators, and swimming pools. Now I dream cabins.

It pops up now and then as a real possibility. A flyer arrives in the mailbox, luring buyers to invest in an idyllic community tucked in some remote and perfect mountain town. We could afford that, I think, and stare, entranced, at images of tan, happy hikers. Or a song on the radio spells it out, verse by verse, the words drawing my heart with promises of happiness for the brave, the dreamers who dare to dream.

It's not a bad dream, this longing of mine. Not a dream at all, really – more of an echo. An echo of Eden, of all that was lost and all that will be restored. I imagine it manifests itself in different ways for different people, but I think for all of us there are moments when one particular strain of the song is especially enticing, moments when we stand with the car keys dangling and think seriously about taking off to find it. And it's in those moments that we have to pay close attention. A hair's breadth apart there balance two radically different options: skim the surface, enchanted, and finally fall into Narcissus' pond, or suck in a breath and go deep.

Narcissus, you remember, was pursued by Echo, a nymph, who loved him and followed him haplessly through the woods. He ignored her, rejected her, lived only for himself. Finally, to spite him, an irritated god, Nemesis, cursed Narcissus, leading him to the edge of a still pool. Catching sight of beauty on the mirror of the pond, he was immediately infatuated. He glimpsed, he loved, he couldn't look away. Ignore the echo, stare long enough at a facsimile of goodness and ultimately you wobble right off of firm ground and sink beneath the illusion to a watery death.

But what if we don't settle for the dazzle of the surface? What if we gulp in air and dive down, down, down to the depths, lungs a-bursting, and find the real treasure there at the bottom?

What if we let the echo sing us Home?

Anything good on earth has the potential to be an idol, leading us astray from the best, or conversely, a tutor, leading us to Christ. How often in the Bible angels have to admonish people not to kneel before them! Hey, guy, I'm just the messenger here, they say. It is too easy to worship beauty, love, or excitement in all their various forms and fail to recognize them as glimpses of God. While we scorn the Israelites and their silly golden calf, we too elevate our treasures and bow before them. We see the signpost, *Heaven, 100 miles*, and crowd around to kneel. If we could but learn to look past the sign to the destination, we could gain strength to run a little farther.

The dream of Home is the dream of a destination which is real, more real than any place you've ever been. C.S. Lewis might say heaven is 'solider' than the stuff of earth. In *The Great Divorce* Lewis describes flowers that weigh more, solid like gemstones instead of soft and wilting. He describes water you might walk across, and heavenly souls like big friendly giants. This world in its corruption and decay hints at what might have been and what still awaits, but as Paul said, it is more like a tent than a temple. We dwell in Temporary.

Put down this page and look up. Can you fathom that Home is out there somewhere, waiting for you? Give Jesus a holler – 'Hey, Jesus! I can't wait to see it! Put the kettle on, I'll be there soon!' Billy Graham said, 'The Bible has much to say about the brevity of life and the necessity of preparing for eternity. I am convinced that only when a man is prepared to die is he also prepared to live.'[3] Dream of Home, and learn to live.

Learn to see this rattletrap train for what it is, a vehicle speeding to its perfect destination. Your sorrows are only temporary, your joys only a prelude. Life is short, as they say; pray hard.

Learn to see your fellow travelers for what they are, children of the living God or lost souls headed to destruction.[4] How you treat them will echo for eternity. Treasure your loved ones; now you see them, now you don't.

Learn what it is to live life passionately, with urgency, anticipation, and joy. Observe that this world is vain and meaningless, smoke and mirrors, that life under the sun is fraught with complications. But see that it is charged with purpose and aglow

---

3. Billy Graham Evangelistic Association, *Billy Graham: God's Ambassador*. (San Diego: Tehabi Books, 1999), 271.

4. In *The Weight of Glory,* C.S. Lewis writes, "It is a serious thing to live in a society of possible gods and goddesses, to remember that the dullest and most uninteresting person you talk to may one day be a creature which, if you saw it now, you would be strongly tempted to worship, or else a horror and a corruption such as you now meet, if at all, only in a nightmare.... There are no ordinary people. You have never talked to a mere mortal."

with hope. Life in Christ is never in vain, and death, in Christ, has no sting.

As the great preacher liked to say, 'Someday you will read or hear that Billy Graham is dead. Don't you believe a word of it! I shall be more alive then than I am now. I will just have changed my address. I will have gone into the presence of God.'

Learn what it is to worship, really worship, and Whom it is you praise.

He is ruddy and handsome, outstanding among 10,000. He is fierce and terrifying, astride His battle horse with His sword unsheathed, eyes blazing like the sun. He is kindness itself, and Love. He is for you. He sang the world to life in the beginning, He sustains it until the end. He holds the keys of life, the keys of death, the keys of heaven and hell. He sits in perfect beauty, compelling worship, astonishing the hard of heart, amazing the wise, welcoming the childlike. He waits for me, He knows my name.

Hallelujah.

> The earth will soon dissolve like snow,
> The sun forbid to shine,
> But God, who called me here below
> Shall be forever mine.
>
> John Newton

Group Study Guide

Chapter 1: See Eternally

- Where do see evidence of non-Christians having eternity in their hearts?"

- Ecclesiastes 3:11 declares that God has 'set eternity' in our hearts. What are several ways this is true in your experience?

- What line of 'Be Thou My Vision' strikes you most powerfully? Why?

- Telling the stories of David Brainerd, Jim Elliott, and Nate Saint, the author says, 'Giving their lives, they gained the crown of life.' What could you give? What would you gain?

- What are at least two components of eternal perspective? Which is hardest for you to maintain?

- Reread Psalm 90. How does Moses' understanding of the brevity of life affect his prayer life?

- Can you think of several ways eternal perspective might affect our obedience? Our love?

- Our perspective clearly affects the way we weather storms. Read 2 Corinthians 4:16-18. How might it change your experience of trials or crises to meditate on a) God's eternal nature, b) God's omnipresence(God is everywhere), c) God's omnipotence (God is all-powerful), and d) God's omniscience (God knows everything)?

Chapter 2: Worship Wholeheartedly

- In Revelation 2:1-7, Jesus compliments the church at Ephesus for what? What does He hold against them? Compare Jeremiah 2:2 and Matthew 24:9-13. What do the three groups addressed have in common?

- Compare David's 'one thing' in Psalm 27:4 with Jesus' 'greatest commandment' in Mark 12:30. Are they the same?

- What does the Bible have to say about living from the heart? Why do you think God prioritizes our heart condition so highly?

- The author says, 'let your life flow from the love of God, live in a way that enhances your love of God, or wither.' In what ways have you set up a life that contributes to your love of God? In what ways does your life distract from or diminish your love of God?

- Think of someone you have known or known about who loves God wholeheartedly. What effect does this love have on his or her life?

- What characteristic of God is demonstrated by His desire for our love and worship?

- Think about the areas of life Jesus mentions in Mark 12:30: He wants us to love Him heart, soul, mind, and strength. How can you measure your love level in each of these areas? What needs shoring up?

Chapter 3: Walk Purposefully

- Have you ever been in a season of overwork? What was going on in your heart during that time?

- Take some time to read John 14-17. This incredible passage records one of Jesus' final conversations with the disciples prior to the cross, including the famous 'high priestly prayer' of chapter 17. Notice the recurring not-of-this-world theme. Jot down verses you see relating to this idea.

- What consolations does Jesus offer His disciples as He prepares to leave this world?

- What seem to be His reasons for leaving the disciples here?

- What commands does He repeat throughout this chapter for the disciples' remaining time on earth?

- We tend to speak of the 'calling' of missionaries and ministers, but what about everyone else? What is your calling?

- Think creatively about the job you currently have. How can you glorify God in that role by doing your job with excellence? How does your vocation have inherent redemptive possibilities for an image-bearer of the Lord?

Chapter 4: Care Passionately

- Compare Isaiah 1:10-20 with Isaiah 58:6-14. What theme does the prophet introduce in Chapter 1 that is restated in Chapter 58? What attitude does Isaiah condemn?

- Both Isaiah 1 and Isaiah 58 contain a series of if/ then statements: If people do this, then God will respond by doing that. List the if/then statements you see in these two chapters.

- Isaiah mentions Sodom and Gomorrah. What was the sin of Sodom, which resulted in the city's destruction? (See Gen. 18-19, and especially, Ezek. 16:49-50.) Does Ezekiel's summary of Sodom's sin surprise you?

- How might having compassion contribute to having an abundant life?

- What is the opposite of love? Explain. Could you make a case for several different possible answers to this question? Is it ever easier for you to choose one of these opposites of love when interacting with the 'lost and least of these'?

- What connection is made between eternal perspective and compassion in the following passages?

    Matthew 25:31-46
    Romans 14:10
    1 John 4:16-21

- When resources such as time and money are limited, how should we decide when and where to offer compassion or care for the poor? How does our obligation change dependent upon the recipient's integrity, lifestyle, level of need, previous gifts received, or attitude?

- How have you seen compassion lead to abundant life in your own life?

Chapter 5: Give Generously

- What attributes of God are reflected by generous Christians (in addition to generosity)?

- In 2 Corinthians 9:6-15, Paul lists several intended results of God's abounding grace to us. What are they?

- If Jesus showed up on your doorstep and handed you $1 million, then vanished, how would you invest it for His Kingdom? How would you decide? Do you feel more or less freedom to spend your paycheck than money personally handed you by God? Why or why not?

- 'Giving generously, in the way that will add to your joy in life, means daydreaming before you give.' Daydream a little now. How could you bless someone in Jesus' name today?

- How is giving generously an echo of the gospel? (Rom. 8:32, John 3:16)

- What did the author mean by 'grace is a burglar that respects no locks'? Do you agree?

- Read Psalm 24. How is God described? And in John 1:12, how are we described? How would a deep understanding of these passages affect our giving practices?

- In what ways have you observed the church's generosity affecting the world? What could result if we went the extra mile?

Chapter 6: Hold Loosely

- How do the following individuals exemplify the principle of holding loosely? What did they give, and what did they gain?

- Abraham (Genesis 22)

- Hannah (1 Samuel 1-2)

- Paul (Philippians 3:4-11)

- The thought of loosening our grip on what we hold dear can be downright terrifying. Does surrender lead to joy? Can we by clinging to something preserve it for our pleasure?

- What if God takes away something or someone we love, permanently? Is this a mean-spirited response to our faith? How can we interpret His actions when we lose someone we love?

- Hebrews 10:19–11:40 speaks to the kind of faith God desires from us and illustrates this steadfast faith with stories of Abraham (and others). According to this passage, what are at least three reasons for our hope? How is faith proportional to or affected by our eternal perspective?

- Psalm 37:4 says, 'Delight yourself in the Lord, and he will give you the desires of your heart.' What would it look like to delight yourself in the Lord, or as Tozer says, to make Jesus your treasure? How would this help you to hold loosely?

Chapter 7: Love Deeply

- Grab a pen and mark all occurrences of the word 'love' in the slim book of I John. Jot down the who-what-when-where-why and hows of this command as listed by John, along with any promises or consequences attached to loving or not loving. Now grade yourself. What would your love report card say about how you are doing with this command?

- Read 1 Corinthians 13 for a more comprehensive description of love. What verbs define love? How's the quality of love that you offer, specifically to other believers in your church and other members of your family?

- Think about someone in your life who is difficult to love. Do you suppose Jesus ever encountered someone like this person? How would He have loved them? What does He expect from you in this relationship? What does He not expect?

- Many Christians have been deeply hurt by other believers, sometimes by the local church itself. What does love look like in that context? How might love practically work itself out in a body of imperfect believers?

- How does the notion that life is fleeting affect your perspective on loving others? Does it affect all of your relationships or only those closest to you?

- Do you agree with the author's statement, 'The chief end of marriage is to glorify God by enjoying Him together'? Could the same be said of friendship? If an outsider observed your marriage or closest friendship, would he or she conclude that the main purpose of that relationship is to enjoy God together?

How could a goal of enjoying God together change your relationships?

- John 17:23 expresses a missional goal to flow out of our love and unity. How do you see this result in the lives of believers?

Chapter 8: Stand Firm

• Think about your church and your personal life from the perspective of the devil. What could he do to cause the most havoc in your community, your family, or your own soul? Why might he attack you?

• What lies has the devil used most frequently to paralyze you? What weak spots does he go after? Ask a close friend or family member to help you identify these if you are having trouble. Oftentimes we can't see our own areas of struggle clearly. For each lie that you list, find a corresponding Biblical passage that counterattacks with truth.

• Colossians 1:9-12 records a mighty prayer of Paul for all followers of Christ to be strengthened in power. In verses 13-16, Paul proclaims, 'He has delivered us from the domain of darkness and transferred us to the kingdom of his beloved Son, in whom we have redemption, the forgiveness of sins. He is the image of the invisible God, the firstborn of all creation. For by him all things were created, in heaven and on earth, visible and invisible, whether thrones or dominions or rulers or authorities – all things were created through him and for him.' According to this passage, how much power is Satan allowed in the lives of believers? How does this passage encourage you?

• In Ephesians 6, Paul lists the following pieces of spiritual armor: the belt of truth, the breastplate of righteousness, the shoes of the gospel of peace, the shield of faith, the helmet of salvation, and the sword of the Spirit. Elsewhere in Scripture, similar but slightly variant imagery pops up. Compare the language of Ephesians 6 with the battle metaphors in these passages: 2 Samuel 22, 1 Thessalonians 5:8, Romans 13:12, Isaiah 59:16-17, Isaiah 49:2, and Hebrews 4:12. Do these passages expand or challenge your understanding of Ephesians 6 in any way? And in Psalm 144, what connection does David make between spiritual battle and eternal perspective?

- How does Paul conclude his discussion of spiritual battle in Ephesians 6:18-20? How important are these concluding verses to this chapter as a whole?

- Does the idea that an invisible spiritual realm surrounds us encourage or frighten you? Why? How did this understanding affect David in 2 Samuel 5? Elijah's servant in 2 Kings 6:11-18? Jesus in the Garden of Gethsemane?

- How might you, in the words of Jim Elliot, be more 'dangerous' this week?

Chapter 9: Choose Light

- In Matthew 6:22-23, Jesus says 'if your eye is healthy, your whole body will be full of light, but if your eye is bad, your whole body will be full of darkness.' What is a 'healthy' eye? In what sense can a person's life be full of light?

- Is treasuring something the same as idolatry? Why or why not?

- How can thankfulness rescue us from idolatry?

- How can gratitude transform difficult circumstances?

- The author writes, 'If you have no words to give thanks, borrow some.' What Scripture, song, or quotation encourages you most in this area of choosing light?

- Colossians 3:1 says, 'set your hearts on things above,' (NIV) while II Corinthians 4:18 admonishes us to fix our eyes on what is unseen and eternal. Is it possible to be, as the cliche would have it, 'so heavenly minded that you are no earthly good'? How would it affect your daily life and choices to meditate on heaven more frequently?

Chapter 10: Rest

- Seven times in the gospel of John, Jesus declares, 'I am the _____.' Read these statements:

- John 6:35,48, 51 'I am the _____.'

- John 8:12 'I am the _____.'

- John 10:7,9 'I am the _____.'

- John 10:11,14 'I am the _____.'

- John 11:25 'I am the _____.'

- John 14:6 'I am the _____.'

- John 15:1,5 'I am the _____.'

- Reread Psalm 23 in light of Jesus' seven 'I am' statements. Is there any overlap between David's metaphors and Jesus'? Do these word pictures work together to give you a fuller understanding of Jesus? What do each of these statements say about Jesus' job and our own roles?

- How does Psalm 23 encourage you to rest?

- Look at Hebrews 4:1-11. How does the author of Hebrews seem to define rest? What special rest awaits the people of God (verse 9)?

- How do the concepts of eternal rest and weekly Sabbath connect?

- What rationale does God give for the institution of the Sabbath in Exodus 20:8-11? What reason does He give in Deuteronomy 5:12-15? How do these two reasons reflect the Great Commandment – to love God and to love your neighbor? How would a community committed to weekly Sabbath contribute to social justice?

- Jesus said, 'Come to me, all who labor and are heavy laden, and I will give you rest' (Matt. 11:28). How have you obeyed this command?

- Why is rest important to your well-being? In what ways do you feel that you need to change the quality or quantity of your rest (daily, weekly, monthly, annually)?

- Over a lifetime, how would a lifestyle of regular stillness and Sabbath-keeping affect your soul? Your family? Your joy?

Chapter 11: Unhooked and Unhindered

- Define, in your own words, 'freedom in Christ.'

- Think of the godliest people you know. Have you observed that they are 'unhooked and unhindered'?

- Our relationship to possessions can be free and fluid, but as Jesus implied, money – or 'stuff' – can quickly become an idol. Is there anything you own that you cling to and could not part with? Is there anything you crave with envy? How have you experienced 'freedom from stuff'?

- Why does Jesus say that it is easier for a camel to thread a needle than a rich man to enter heaven?

- In language similar to Hebrews 12, Proverbs 5:22 says, 'An evil man is held captive by his own sins; they are ropes that catch and hold him' (NLT). How have you allowed sin to entangle you in the past? What were the results?

- What sins do you tend to tolerate or justify, 'in the name of authenticity, perhaps'?

- Read Galatians 5. If it is not by following the law that we achieve holiness, how can we? How does this chapter of Galatians seem to define freedom in Christ?

- In what ways can fear hamper true freedom? How does the hope of heaven contribute to a life of freedom in Christ?

- How can you cultivate childlike freedom to approach God in prayer?

Chapter 12: Home

- 'When you desire something pure and perfect here on earth, recognize it for what it is, a signpost pointing you on your way. In itself, it cannot satisfy your soul. But does it reflect the love, creativity, holiness, and goodness of God? Look up, see perfection Himself, and worship.' List three or four things on earth that you find yourself longing for. In what ways do these specific things point you Home?

- In what ways do you think our dreams are echoes of Eden? Take a minute to reread Genesis 1–3. What was true of Eden, of Adam's and Eve's lives, before the fall? And after? What hints do you see in this passage of God's intentions towards us? What has Satan's scheme towards us always been?

- What do you think of Billy Graham's statement, 'only when a man is prepared to die is he also prepared to live'?

- If Heaven consisted of everything delightful, beautiful, and exciting that you could imagine, but was without Jesus, would you want to go there? (You will probably say no to this question, knowing that it's the right thing to say. But deep down, do you struggle with that answer? Why would a Heaven without Jesus be Hell? How does the Hollywood version of Heaven fall short?)

- If you knew that tomorrow you would wake up in Heaven, what would change for you today?

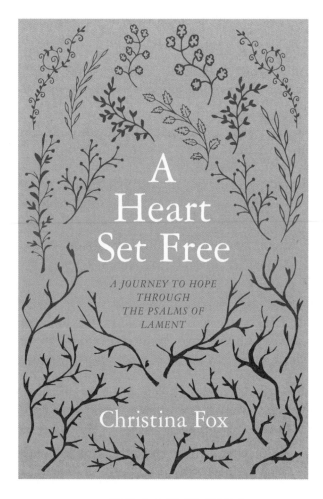

A
Heart
Set Free

*A JOURNEY TO HOPE
THROUGH
THE PSALMS OF
LAMENT*

Christina Fox

ISBN 978-1-78191-728-2

A Heart Set Free
A Journey to Hope through the Psalms of Lament
CHRISTINA FOX

For many of us, we might busy ourselves with projects or work long hours to keep our mind off our pain. We might look at our circumstances and seek to change our situation in the hope that we will finally feel at peace once our life has changed.

The question is - How often do you look to God in His Word for help and hope? How often do you turn to Him when you feel anxious, distraught, or abandoned? How often do you bring your burdens to your Savior? Take a journey of hope through the Psalms of lament with Christina Fox.

Some days feel like a roller coaster ride--up and down, and if possible sideways ... Christina doesn't ignore our emotions, rather she drives us from the wild ride to the freedom found in Jesus.

Trillia Newbell
Author of *Fear and Faith* and *United*

... I wish I had Christina's book back when I became a believer. It would have saved me a lot of painful emotion-stuffing and foolish emotion-ignoring.

Gloria Furman
Author of *Glimpses of Grace, Treasuring Christ When Your Hands Are Full,* and *The Pastor's Wife*

Christina Fox is a blogger at www.christinafox.com where she chronicles her faith journey. She writes for a number of Christian ministries and publications including Desiring God and The Gospel Coalition. She lives with her husband and two sons in Roswell, Georgia.

Christian Focus Publications

Our mission statement –

STAYING FAITHFUL
In dependence upon God we seek to impact the world through literature faithful to His infallible Word, the Bible. Our aim is to ensure that the Lord Jesus Christ is presented as the only hope to obtain forgiveness of sin, live a useful life and look forward to heaven with Him.

Our books are published in four imprints:

CHRISTIAN
FOCUS

Popular works including biographies, commentaries, basic doctrine and Christian living.

CHRISTIAN
HERITAGE

Books representing some of the best material from the rich heritage of the church.

MENTOR

Books written at a level suitable for Bible College and seminary students, pastors, and other serious readers. The imprint includes commentaries, doctrinal studies, examination of current issues and church history.

CF4•K

Children's books for quality Bible teaching and for all age groups: Sunday school curriculum, puzzle and activity books; personal and family devotional titles, biographies and inspirational stories – Because you are never too young to know Jesus!

Christian Focus Publications Ltd,
Geanies House, Fearn, Ross-shire,
IV20 1TW, Scotland, United Kingdom.
www.christianfocus.com